The American Empire and the Commonwealth of God

A Political, Economic, Religious Statement

David Ray Griffin
John B. Cobb Jr.
Richard A. Falk
Catherine Keller

Westminster John Knox Press
LOUISVILLE • LONDON

Book design by Sharon Adams
Cover design by designpointinc.com

First edition
Published by Westminster John Knox Press
Louisville, Kentucky

This book is printed on acid-free paper that meets the American National Standards Institute Z39.48 standard. ♾

PRINTED IN THE UNITED STATES OF AMERICA

06 07 08 09 10 11 12 13 14 15—10 9 8 7 6 5 4 3 2

Library of Congress Cataloging-in-Publication Data

The American empire and the commonwealth of God : a political, economic, religious statement / David Ray Griffin . . . [et al.]—1st ed.
    p. cm.
Includes bibliographical references.
ISBN-13: 978-0-664-23009-8
ISBN-10: 0-664-23009-1
1. Christianity and politics—United States—Congresses. 2. Christianity and international affairs—Congresses. 3. United States—Foreign relations—Philosophy—Congresses. 4. Imperialism—Congresses. I. Griffin, David Ray, 1939–

BR526.E95 2006
261.8'7—dc22

2005058477

Contents

Preface

We have produced this book on the basis of several shared convictions. One of these is that we live in a time that is without precedent in two respects. For the first time since the rise of human civilization, the history of which has to a large extent been a history of empires, one empire is now on the verge of becoming a truly global empire, an empire with no borders. For the first time as well, we are aware that even if the human race avoids self-annihilation through nuclear weapons, it is on a trajectory toward self-annihilation through human-caused climate change. These two crises are, moreover, closely related, because the nation that is seeking to become the world's first borderless empire—the United States of America—is also the nation that, precisely through its imperialist policies, is the primary threat to the survival of the human species (along with that of many other species as well).

We have written this book in order to register our protest against this empire and also to argue that there is no reason to accept the emergence of a global *Pax Americana* as inevitable, because there *is* a better alternative.

We oppose the American empire on political, economic, and ecological grounds. We believe that on all these grounds, this empire is bad for the world and even bad for America and Americans.

We also strongly oppose this empire on religious-spiritual-moral grounds. Our convictions here have been shaped by the major faith traditions of the world, including those from non-Western civilizations, especially by the biblical tradition in general and by the message of Jesus of Nazareth in particular. Although it might seem initially strange that this would be true of all of us, since one of us (Richard Falk) is Jewish, it is in fact not strange at all: The legacy of Jesus belongs to the whole of humanity, as does that of Muhammad and Gautama the Buddha. Besides, Jesus was a Jew; he had a thoroughly Jewish vision of reality; he stood in the tradition of the great Hebrew prophets, such as Amos, Hosea, Isaiah, and Jeremiah; and his message, which was a profoundly anti-imperialist message, was proclaimed on behalf of his people, and in the name of their God, at a time when their land was occupied by the brutal and idolatrous Roman Empire. His concern for a "reign of God," in the sense of a world in which God's will is carried out in our personal, political, and economic relationships, is a concern common to all three of the Abrahamic traditions. We oppose the American empire on the basis of what we believe to be the sacred, divinely rooted moral law of the universe.

Another common element in our religious visions is the conviction that insofar as the dominant image of the Divine Reality has been easily used to support empire, this image is profoundly wrong, even idolatrous. This use is illustrated by a rhetorical question contained in the Christmas card sent out by Vice President Cheney in 2003: "And if a sparrow cannot fall to the ground without His notice, is it probable that an empire can rise without His aid?"[1]

We are supported in this conviction by another element we have in common, the influence of the philosophy of Alfred North Whitehead. Given the origin of the Jesus movement as an anti-imperial movement, which contrasted the reign of God to the reign of Caesar, it would have been one of the greatest reversals in history if the God of this movement, which came to be called Christianity, had been given the attributes of Caesar, thereby declaring divine the kind of power wielded by emperors—the power to coerce, destroy, and kill. And yet, as Whitehead pointed out (see chapter 7), this is exactly what happened. We agree with Whitehead that not only Christianity but all religious-moral movements, insofar as they distinguish what *is* from what *ought to be* and also promote nonviolent means of bringing about what ought to be, need a view of deity that does not imply divine sanction either for violence or for the present order.

We also share the conviction that the Bush-Cheney administration has played a revelatory role, making evident to large numbers of people what in prior times had been detected by only a few observers, namely, that the United States has long been working toward the goal of exercising unchallenged and exploitative control of the planet. Its currently declared policy of preventive-preemptive war, while demonstrating a new level of contempt for international law and morality (see chapters 3 and 4), is simply a new method for eliminating regimes that resist its rule and for enlarging its empire of military bases and its control of the world's natural resources.

We also find the revelatory role of this administration to extend to the motives behind this goal, because the Bush-Cheney administration has made abundantly clear to anyone with eyes to see and ears to hear—and perhaps no corporate profits to protect—the enormous gap between its professed and actual motives. In doing so, however, the Bush-Cheney administration has only made more evident the gap that has long existed between the rhetoric and the reality of U.S. foreign policy, as illustrated in many of this book's chapters.

We also share the conviction that the long-discussed question about global governance—whether it would be desirable—has been superseded by events. The only question now is whether it would be better for global governance to be exercised by an imperial power that has imposed its policies on the rest of the world, or by institutions freely set up by the peoples of the world to run the world on democratic principles. We have written this book to emphasize that these are now the alternatives we confront.

Apologists for the Bush-Cheney administration, to be sure, suggest that we need not choose between global empire and global democracy, because the unique thing about the American empire is that it is dedicated to the spread of democracy. We, however, find nothing in the history of U.S. foreign policy in general or that of the Bush-Cheney administration in particular to lend cred-ibility to this conceit. We instead hold that unless the peoples of the world want to see a further extension and intensification of the present form of global governance, with its combination of plutocracy and imperialism, it is time to begin devising means through which the world can be *genuinely* democra-tized, both politically and economically.

We recognize that replacing the present global order, which is based on violence and other modes of coercion, with a world based on democratic prin-ciples will be a shift of enormous magnitude, in some ways the greatest trans-formation since the beginning of civilization itself. We recognize, moreover, that like all previous fundamental shifts, this one will require a vision that is religious (or spiritual) as well as political and economic. We have, accord-ingly, sought to show that such a threefold vision already exists.

The remainder of the book consists of chapters written by one or the other of us as individuals. Over the years, however, we have all in many ways, including through many conferences, learned from each other. So, even though none of us may fully endorse every detail in our colleagues' chapters, we all felt comfortable with affixing our names to the book as a whole.

Earlier versions of chapters 1–6 were presented at a conference on Amer-ican Empire sponsored by the Center for Process Studies and held at the Clare-mont School of Theology, October 4–5, 2003. Earlier versions of chapters 7 and 8 and a still earlier version of chapters 1 and 6 were presented at a con-ference on American Empire at Drew University Theological School, Sep-tember 25–27, 2003. An earlier version of chapter 9 was published in *Creative Transformation* 13/4 (Fall 2004).

David Ray Griffin, John B. Cobb Jr., Richard Falk, and Catherine Keller

PART I

The Nature of
the American Empire

Chapter 1

America's Non-Accidental, Non-Benign Empire

David Ray Griffin

*T*he idea of an "American empire," along with the related idea of "American imperialism," has had an interesting history. In the nineteenth century, the idea was openly discussed, even celebrated. The reigning assumption was that the emerging American empire, unlike all previous empires, would be a benign, even a benevolent, empire. It would be an "empire of liberty," bringing freedom wherever it spread. In the twentieth century, however, the term "imperialism" acquired such negative connotations that politicians and even respectable intellectuals ceased speaking of American imperialism, except to deny its existence. In 1983, for example, President Ronald Reagan declared, "We're not in the business of imperialism, aggression or conquest. . . . We threaten no one."[1]

The negative connotations of the word "imperialism," moreover, spread to the word "empire," so that at the very time the United States was creating the most extensive empire the world had ever known, politicians and respectable intellectuals had to deny that there *was* an American empire.

The main rationale for denying the existence of an American empire was the equation of empire with the kind of *colonial* empire Great Britain had. By making that equation and then overlooking the awkward fact that America did have a few formal colonies, American leaders could deny that they ruled over an ever-growing empire. This ploy ignored the fact that American business and political leaders had made a conscious decision to create a different kind of empire: a *neocolonial* empire, sometimes called an *informal* empire. As Ludwell Denny said in 1930, "We shall not make Britain's mistake. Too wise to try to govern the world, we shall merely own it."[2] By "merely" owning countries, without having formal colonial offices, American could sustain the myth, at least among its own people, that it was not an imperial power.

Although politicians and most respectable intellectuals supported this myth, a few intellectuals, while admitting the existence of an American empire, remained respectable by stipulating that America's empire differed from all previous empires in two respects. First, America acquired its empire *accidentally*. This idea is illustrated by Ernest May's 1961 study, *Imperial Democracy: The Emergence of America as a Great Power*. "Some nations achieve greatness," said May, but "the United States had greatness thrust upon it."[3]

The second defense of the American empire was that, unlike all previous empires, it is *benign*. A classic statement of this view can be found in a 1967 book by Ronald Steel entitled *Pax Americana*. Writing as the criticism of the Vietnam War was heating up, Steel acknowledged that "by any conventional standards for judging such things," America is "an imperial power," having an empire "the scope of which the world has never seen."[4] However, Steel argued, "America has been engaged in a kind of welfare imperialism, empire building for noble ends rather than for such base motives as profit and influence"—the chief noble end being "permitting other nations to enjoy the benefits of freedom, democracy, and self-determination."[5] When America intervenes, Steel said, it does so with "the most noble motives and with the most generous impulses."[6]

The most effective way to show the falsity of these views—that America has no empire or that, if it does, its empire is an accidental, benign empire— would be to rehearse the story of U.S. imperialism.

But this would be a very long story. It would need to begin with the displacement of the Native Americans, which involved the extermination of about ten million of them.[7] It would need to include the institution of slavery, which, besides all the other evils, probably involved the deaths of another ten million human beings.[8] This story would need to explain why in 1829 the South American hero Simon Bolivar said, "It seems to be the destiny of the United States to impoverish [the rest of] America." This story would need to deal with the theft of what is now the American Southwest from Mexico.[9] It would need to deal with the increasing number of invasions after the American Civil War in countries such as Guatemala, El Salvador, Chile, Brazil, and Venezuela.[10] It would need to deal with the so-called Spanish-American Wars of 1898–1902, during which America took control of Cuba, Puerto Rico, the Philippines, Hawaii, and Guam.[11] It would need to explain why the war to deny independence to the Filipinos led to the formation of the Anti-Imperialist League, with one of its members, William James, saying: "God damn the U.S. for its vile conduct in the Philippine Isles."[12] This story of American imperialism would also need to tell of America's interventions further abroad—in Japan in 1854, China in 1900, Russia in 1918, and Hungary in 1919.[13] Back in this hemisphere, this story would need to tell of America's theft of Panama from Colombia in 1903, then its repeated interventions in the Dominican Republic, Haiti, Nicaragua, Costa Rica, Guatemala, and El Salvador, with lengthy occupations of some of those countries.[14] It would need to explain its imperial aims in World War II, which led it to install right-wing governments in Greece, France, Italy, Japan, Korea, and the Philippines, even though this meant turning against the Resistance movements, which had fought alongside the Allies against the Fascist powers.[15] This story would then need to explain, against deeply entrenched mythology, how the Cold War was far more the result of the imperial ambitions of the United States than those of the Soviet Union.[16] It would also need to tell of the great number of countries in which the United States overthrew constitutional governments, such as Iran (1953), Guatemala (1954), Brazil (1961–64), the Dominican Republic (1965), Greece (1965 and 1967), Indonesia (1965–66), and Chile (1973), as well as its later interventions in Nicaragua and El Salvador.[17] This story of U.S. imperialism would need to describe America's thirty-year effort to prevent the unification and independence of Vietnam, a process that also involved merciless bombings of Laos and Cambodia.[18] It would then need to tell of the policies that have led to such hatred of America in the Arab and Muslim worlds.[19] This story would need, furthermore, to tell of other dimensions of U.S. imperialism, such as the economic policies behind these interventions (some of which will be described in John Cobb's chapters) and America's posture with regard to nuclear weapons (as described in Richard Falk's first chapter).[20]

So, although telling this story would be the most effective way to argue that America's empire is neither accidental nor benign, this obviously cannot be done within the confines of a chapter. However, there is now a quicker way to make this case, thanks to the publication in 2002 of a book by Andrew Bacevich entitled *American Empire*.[21] Bacevich is a conservative. But he is an *honest* conservative, who tells the truth about the American empire, pointing out that it is neither accidental nor benign.

There have, of course, been previous intellectuals who have told these truths, but they have been left-leaning thinkers, such as Charles Beard, Noam Chomsky, Richard Falk, Walter LaFeber, William Appleton Williams, and Howard Zinn.[22] Their account of the American empire could be easily dismissed by mainline thinkers as distorted by a left-wing agenda.

Bacevich, however, has no such agenda. We can assume, therefore, that insofar as his account contradicts the standard denial of the existence of an American empire and the standard portrayal of this empire as accidental and benign, it is not distorted by ideological bias.

The Reality of the American Empire

As Bacevich points out, it is still considered impolitic for those in office to admit to the existence of an American empire. In his West Point speech in June of 2002, President Bush said, "We don't seek an empire." Likewise, when Secretary of Defense Donald Rumsfeld was asked by an al-Jazeera correspondent in 2003 if the Bush administration was bent on "empire-building," Rumsfeld replied, "We don't seek empires. We're not imperialistic. We never have been. I can't imagine why you'd even ask the question."[23] But many imperialists who are outside the government no longer feel the need to deny the obvious.

For example, in 2000, Richard Haass, soon to become the director of policy planning in Colin Powell's State Department, gave an address titled "Imperial America," in which he called on Americans to "re-conceive their global role from one of a traditional nation-state to an imperial power."[24] In January of 2001, Robert Kagan criticized "Clinton and his advisers" for "having the stomach only to be halfway imperialists."[25]

Only after September 11, 2001, however, did the language of empire become really prominent. Early in 2002, columnist Charles Krauthammer wrote: "People are coming out of the closet on the word 'empire.'" Believing this a good thing, Krauthammer said that Americans need to face up to responsibilities entailed by the fact that they are now "undisputed masters of the world."[26]

Bacevich himself provides the ultimate example of this new willingness of conservatives to admit the obvious. Against those who still try to pretend that America is not the head of a worldwide empire, Bacevich says:

> Holding sway in not one but several regions of pivotal geopolitical importance, disdaining the legitimacy of political economic principles other than its own, declaring the existing order to be sacrosanct, asserting unquestioned military supremacy with a globally deployed force configured not for self-defense but for coercion: these are the actions of a nation engaged in the governance of empire.[27]

Some of these imperialists are quite frank in their advocacy of the unilateral use of American power. In an essay in the *Atlantic Monthly* in 2003, Robert Kaplan publicly argued that America should use its power unilaterally to "manage an unruly world," leaving behind "the so-called international community" and especially the United Nations, whose Security Council "represents an antiquated power arrangement unreflective of the latest wave of U.S. military modernization."[28] Richard Perle says that the Bush administration has already brought about this change. In a commentary entitled "Thank God for the Death of the UN," Perle says, "Its abject failure gave us only anarchy. The world needs order." That order is to be provided, of course, by the United States.[29]

The American Empire as Non-Accidental

This new openness about the reality of the American empire by its supporters is generally coupled, however, with what Bacevich calls the "The Myth of the Reluctant Superpower," according to which "greatness was not sought; it just happened."[30] In illustrating this myth, he uses Ernest May's previously quoted statement that the United States, without seeking it, "had greatness thrust upon it."[31] In Bacevich's more complete characterization of this myth, he says:

> In this view, American policy is a response to external factors. The United States does not act in accordance with some predetermined logic; it reacts to circumstances. . . . [T]he United States—unlike other nations—achieved pre-eminence not by consciously seeking it but simply as an unintended consequence of actions taken either in self-defense or on behalf of others.[32]

A recent example of this stance appeared in President Bush's address on Veteran's Day, 2005, in which he declared, with regard to the so-called war on terror, "We didn't ask for this global struggle, but we're answering history's call with confidence."[33]

Bacevich himself, he admits, had previously accepted this myth. He had assumed that American foreign policy was actually guided by its stated objectives, which were "quite limited—to protect our homeland, to preserve our values, to defend our closest allies."[34] On the basis of this assumption, he believed that the American participation in the Cold War was a purely defensive effort to contain Soviet expansionism. He believed that the Soviet Union wanted to establish a worldwide empire but that the United States did not.

He assumed, accordingly, that after winning this war, the United States would greatly reduce its military budget, its weapons programs, and its overseas deployments. But instead, he says,

> in the decade following the fall of the Berlin Wall, . . . [t]he United States employed military power not merely in response to a crisis. . . . It did so to . . . anticipate, intimidate, preempt . . . and control. And it did so routinely and continuously. In the age of globalization, the Department of Defense completed its transformation into a Department of Power Projection.[35]

More generally, he reports, the objectives of U.S. foreign policy "aimed at nothing short of a full-scale transformation of the international order." Realizing that he had been operating with faulty assumptions, Bacevich began his rethinking of what American foreign policy was all about by delving into the works of two leftist critics of U.S. policy, Charles Beard and William Appleton Williams. According to Beard, America intervened abroad not selflessly to help others but to advance its own commercial empire.[36] Besides coming to accept this view, Bacevich also came to agree with the basic point of Williams's view about the American empire—that, far from just having grown "like Topsy," it "emerged out of a particular worldview and reflected a coherent strategy."[37] The scope of this "grand strategy," which "has not changed in a century," adds Bacevich, "is nothing short of stupendous."[38]

So America did not acquire its worldwide empire accidentally, but by means of a consciously formulated strategy, which was executed about equally by Republican and Democratic administrations for well over a century.

The American Empire as Non-Benign

The idea that America acquired its empire accidentally is usually a subordinate point, made to support a claim more crucial to the defense of America's imperial role—namely, that it is benign.

The Empire as Benign

I earlier quoted Ronald Steel's 1967 statement of this view. But, as I intimated earlier, this idea extends back to the founding of the nation and even before. In *The Rising American Empire*, Richard Van Alstyne reports that "before the middle of the eighteenth century, the concept of an empire that would take in the whole continent was fully formed."[39] From the outset, moreover, the idea of the American empire as an "empire of liberty," hence an "empire of right," was repeatedly articulated. For example, a poem by David Humphreys, a protégé of George Washington's, included these lines:

> Our constitutions form'd on freedom's base,
> Which all the blessings of all lands embrace;
> Embrace humanity's extended cause,
> A world of our empire, for a world of our laws.[40]

America's cause, in other words, is identical with humanity's cause, which is freedom. This claim, which has since been repeated countless times, was reiterated in President Bush's address to the nation on September 7, 2003. Defending his policy in Iraq, he closed his address by saying, "We are serving in freedom's cause, a cause that is the cause of all mankind." Given this identity, the spread of the American empire will be a blessing for all.

This idea has been most characteristically expressed in the phrase "manifest destiny," which was coined in 1845.[41] Although originally the phrase referred only to the mission of the United States "to overspread the continent," an editor named Debow wrote in 1850:

> We have a destiny to perform, a "manifest destiny" over all Mexico, over South America, over the West Indies and Canada. . . . The gates of the Chinese empire must be thrown down. . . . The eagle of the republic shall poise itself over the field of Waterloo . . . and a successor of Washington ascend the chair of universal empire![42]

Debow and others who thought in these terms assumed that other nations should not take offense, because America's universal empire would be a "democratic empire." Although America would, like previous great nations, exercise imperialism, it would be a "New Imperialism," one "destined to carry world-wide the principles of Anglo-Saxon peace and justice, liberty and law."[43]

As I mentioned earlier, in the twentieth century, as the negative connotations that accrued to the word "imperialism" tainted the word "empire," this kind of talk became infrequent. Although the old notion of America as a benign empire was still occasionally articulated, as illustrated by Steel's *Pax Americana*, most defenders of American policy simply denied, at least by omission, that America had an empire of any sort.

After the crumbling of the Soviet Union, however, the idea of America as a benign imperial power began to be stated more frequently. In a widely cited 1990 essay, "The Unipolar Moment," Charles Krauthammer said that although people usually recoil "at the thought of a single dominant power for fear of what it will do with its power. . . [,] America is the exception to this rule," because "the world generally sees it as benign," as a power that "acts not just out of self-interest but a sense of right."[44] In 1998, Robert Kagan published an essay entitled "The Benevolent Empire."[45] In 2001, Krauthammer wrote, "[W]e are not just any hegemon. We run a uniquely benign imperium. This is not mere self-congratulation; it is a fact manifest in the way others welcome our power." In 2002, Dinesh D'Souza, after saying that "America has become an empire," added that happily it is "the most magnanimous imperial power ever."[46] In 2003, Krauthammer again asserted that America's claim to being a benign power is not mere "self-congratulation," because the truth of this claim is verified by America's "track record."[47] Michael Ignatieff, in that same year, wrote, "America's empire is not like empires of times past, built on . . . conquest. . . . [It] is a new invention . . . , an empire lite, a global hegemony whose grace notes are free markets, human rights and democracy. . . . It is the imperialism of . . . good intentions."[48] Having written this essay to defend military intervention in Iraq, Ignatieff said that America's good intentions include the aim to replace dictatorships with democracies. In 2005, Krauthammer said that "the strengthening and spread of democracy" is "[t]he great project of the Bush administration."[49] The day before, in the inaugural address for his second term, President Bush himself said that "the policy of the United States [is] to seek and support the growth of democratic movements and institutions in every nation and culture."[50]

The Empire as Not Benign

Bacevich agrees with these men that it is good to be forthright about the existence of the American empire. But he rejects their attempt to justify this empire by claiming that America's intentions are benign. He dismisses, for example, the conceit that "the United States [has] fought [in wars] for altruistic purposes, seeking to end war itself and to make the world safe for democracy."[51] He ridicules the claim "that the promotion of peace, democracy, and human rights and the punishment of evil-doers—*not* the pursuit of self-interest—[has] defined the essence of American diplomacy." And he rejects the claim that "[t]o the extent that interests [have] figured at all, . . . American interests and American ideals [have been] congruent."[52]

Bacevich speaks instead of "the unflagging self-interest and large ambitions underlying all U.S. policy" and of the aim of the U.S. military "to achieve something approaching omnipotence: 'Full Spectrum Dominance.'"[53] He mocks the claim that while such power wielded by others would be threatening, "it is by definition benign" in America's hands because the leader of the free world "does not exploit or dominate but acts on behalf of purposes that look beyond mere self-interest."[54] Bacevich knows that time and time again the U.S. government has intervened to dominate and exploit other countries. Finally, whereas members of the benign-empire school claim that America intervenes in countries such as Iraq in order to promote peace and democracy, Bacevich points out that in previous countries in which America has intervened, "democracy [did not] flower as a result." America intervenes instead "to sustain American primacy."[55] The view of Bacevich the conservative seems not far from Chomsky the radical, who has summed up the effect of U.S. interventions in the title of one of his books, *Deterring Democracy*.[56]

After the world witnessed the Bush administration's response to 9/11, comparisons of America with Rome became commonplace. In 2002, a article appeared in a London newspaper asking "Is America the New Rome?" Saying that "the word of the hour is empire," the author said that "suddenly America is bearing its name."[57] In that same year, Krauthammer wrote that America is "no mere international citizen" but "the dominant power in the world, more dominant than any since Rome."[58]

Bacevich also answers this question in the affirmative. Pointing out that Charles Beard had argued in 1939 that "America is not to be Rome,"[59] Bacevich adds that in the 1990s "most citizens still comforted themselves with the belief that as the sole superpower the United States was *nothing* like Rome." However, Bacevich says: "The reality that Beard feared has come to pass: like it or not, America today *is* Rome."[60]

As Bacevich's comments make clear, this idea includes the point that America is no more benign than Rome. Although Rome's rulers spoke of *Pax Romana*, with one of its emperors assuming the title "Pacifier of the World,"[61] this pacification was achieved by means of its overwhelming military might, which the Romans used ruthlessly. As a Caledonian chieftain at the time put it, the Romans "rob, butcher, plunder, and call it 'empire'; and where they make desolation, they call it 'peace.'"[62]

The Romans used their overwhelming power not merely to conquer but also to terrorize and thereby intimidate their conquered subjects to keep them in line. When the Roman legions were sent on expeditions, accordingly, their main mission was usually "to punish, to avenge, and to terrify—that is, to reassert a certain state of mind in the enemy"—a state of "awe and terror."[63]

America's Move toward Complete Global Dominance

Since the United States became the only superpower, its leaders have expressed rather openly their intention to use their power in a similar way. In 1992, Colin Powell, then head of the Joint Chiefs of Staff, told members of Congress that America requires sufficient power to "deter any challenger from ever dreaming of challenging us on the world stage." Powell even said, "I want to be the bully on the block," implanting in the mind of potential opponents the realization that "there is no future in trying to challenge the armed forces of the United States."[64] It is rather sobering to read these comments in light of the fact that Powell was later, in comparison with others in the administration of George W. Bush, considered a dove.

Also in 1992, in any case, similar ideas were expressed in the draft of the Pentagon's "Defense Planning Guidance" (DPG) document, authored by Paul Wolfowitz, who would become George W. Bush's deputy secretary of defense, and Lewis "Scooter" Libby, who would become Vice President

Cheney's chief of staff. This document said, "Our first objective is to prevent the re-emergence of a new rival. . . . [W]e must maintain the mechanisms for deterring potential competitors from even aspiring to a regional or global role." This document, Bacevich says, "was in effect a blueprint for permanent American global hegemony."[65]

Bacevich, considering Wolfowitz to be the document's primary author, refers to it as "Wolfowitz's Indiscretion" because, instead of using the standard language of American statecraft, promising to use American power "to assure the survival and success of liberty," this document was too candid, "openly suggest[ing] that calculations of power and self-interest rather than altruism and high ideals provided the proper basis for framing strategy."[66] When the document was leaked and portions of it printed in the press, the resulting furor, in which Wolfowitz was "roundly denounced," led the Pentagon to withdraw and rewrite the document.

However, Bacevich points out, its basic ideas would reappear in later documents, including *The National Security Strategy of the United States of America*, published in September 2002. This document, known as *NSS 2002*, said, "We must build and maintain our defenses beyond challenge" so that we can "dissuade future military competition." With statements such as "our best defense is a good offense,"[67] moreover, this document introduced the doctrine of *preventive* warfare, which involves attacking other countries before they pose an immediate threat.

In stating these and related policies, *NSS 2002* was adopting many of the recommendations of a document entitled *Rebuilding America's Defenses*, published in 2000 by the Project for the New American Century, many of the founders of which became central figures in the George W. Bush administration, including Cheney, Libby, Wolfowitz, Richard Armitage, John Bolton, Richard Perle, Donald Rumsfeld, James Woolsey, and Zalmay Khalilzad. Especially noteworthy is the fact that Libby and Wolfowitz, who had coauthored the draft of the 1992 Defense Planning Guidance document, were directly involved in the production of this 2000 document.[68]

Rebuilding America's Defenses emphasizes the importance of greatly increased funding for the technological "revolution in military affairs," at the center of which is the U.S. Space Command.

The U.S. Space Command

The purpose of the Space Command, which is essentially a new branch of the military, is spelled out quite explicitly in a document published in February of 1997 called "Vision for 2020," at the head of which is this mission statement: "U.S. Space Command—dominating the space dimension of military operations to protect US interests and investment."[69] This 1997 document engaged in no sentimental propaganda about the need for the United States to dominate space for the sake of promoting democracy or otherwise serving humanity. It instead said, "The globalization of the world economy . . . will continue with a widening between 'haves' and 'have-nots.'" In other words, although the official line is that U.S.-led economic globalization will make everyone better off, the Pentagon knows that as America's plutocratic domination of the world economy increases, the poor will get still poorer while the rich get still richer. This will make the "have-nots" hate America all the more, so we need to be able to keep them in line.[70] We can do this through "Full Spectrum Dominance," which means not only being dominant on land, on the sea, and in the air, as we are today, but having control of space as well.

This is a three-part program. The only part of it that has received much public discussion is the so-called Missile Defense Shield. A second part, which involves surveillance technology that can zero in on any part of the planet with such precision that every enemy of U.S. forces can be identified, is already well on the way to being realized.[71] The third part involves putting actual weapons in space, including laser cannons, which have the offensive potential, as one writer put it, to "make a cruise missile look like a firecracker."[72] With laser weapons on our satellites, the United States will be able, as the document says, "to deny others the use of space," thereby giving America total and permanent dominance.

Although the U.S. military's intention to weaponize space was previously known only by a few people, it was revealed by Tim Weiner in a *New York Times* front-page story in May 2005.[73] Pointing out that the Air Force is seeking a presidential directive to field "offensive and defensive space weapons," Weiner quotes the head of the Space Command, General Lance Lord, as saying that the goal is "space superiority," defined as "freedom to attack as well as freedom from attack."

We should probably resist the temptation to base a theological critique of this program on the fact that it is headed by a man who is addressed as "General Lord." However, in light of Bacevich's previously quoted observation that the U.S. military has been seeking "to achieve something approaching omnipotence," we can legitimately point out that the name of one of the Space Command's programs, "Rods from God," does suggest that it seeks the kind of destructive omnipotence attributed to God by traditional theists (as emphasized in Catherine Keller's chapter)—destructive power that is intended to be used to dominate other nations. Weiner refers to a strategy called Global Strike, which, according to Lord, will involve the "incredible capability" to destroy things "anywhere in the world . . . in 45 minutes."

The aggressive purpose of the U.S. Space Command's program is announced in the logo of one of its divisions: "In Your Face from Outer Space."[74] Such aggressive, offensive aims are also stated frankly elsewhere. In a book entitled *Full Spectrum Dominance*, Rahul Mahajan points out that *Rebuilding America's Defenses* makes the following "remarkable admission":

> In the post–Cold-War era, America and its allies . . . have become the primary objects of deterrence and it is states like Iraq, Iran and North Korea who most wish to develop deterrent capabilities. Projecting conventional military forces . . . will be far more complex and constrained when the American homeland . . . is subject to attack by otherwise weak rogue regimes capable of cobbling together a minuscule ballistic missile force. Building an effective . . . system of missile defenses is a prerequisite for maintaining American preeminence.[75]

In other words, although the name Missile Defense Shield suggests that the system's purpose is to deter attacks from other nations, its real purpose is to *prevent other nations from deterring America*. If a nation that wishes not to become part of the American empire has a modest number of nuclear missiles, we could eliminate most of them with a first strike. Then if the few surviving ones were launched at the United States, the Missile Defense Shield would be able to intercept them (even though it would probably not be good enough to protect us from a large-scale attack). On this basis, we could take over countries such as North Korea and Iran, even if they have some nuclear weapons.

Advocates of the system have been remarkably willing to admit that the purpose of this "defense" system is offensive. Condoleezza Rice, for example, has said that the purpose of the missile defense system would be to protect America's "freedom of action." Lawrence Kaplan has been even more candid, saying, "Missile defense isn't really meant to protect America. It's a tool for global domination."[76]

Full Spectrum Dominance, which the weaponization of space will provide, is for the sake of completing what Richard Falk has labeled "the global domination project," which he characterizes as "an unprecedented exhibition of geopolitical greed at its worst."[77] A similar judgment would have been made by Adam Smith, who criticized the "vile and selfish maxim of all for ourselves and nothing for other people," which has been followed by "the masters of mankind in every age."[78]

The Bush administration exploited the attacks of 9/11 to get a great increase in funding for the U.S. Space Command. There had been predictions, indeed, that some such event would probably be necessary. In calling for the completion of the "revolution in military affairs," *Rebuilding America's Defenses* said that the needed transformation would probably come about slowly, "absent some catastrophic and catalyzing event—like a new Pearl Harbor."[79] A similar statement is found in the Commission to Assess U.S. National Security Space Management and Organization, which was chaired by Donald Rumsfeld. The report of this Rumsfeld Commission, which was issued in January of 2001 just before Rumsfeld became secretary of defense, recommended the subordination of the other armed forces and all intelligence agencies to the Space Force. Recognizing that such a drastic reorganization would normally evoke great resistance, the report added:

> History is replete with instances in which warning signs were ignored and change resisted until an external, "improbable" event forced resistant bureaucracies to take action. The question is . . . whether, as in the past, a disabling attack against the country and its people—a "Space Pearl Harbor"—will be the only event able to galvanize the nation and cause the U.S. Government to act.[80]

A Space Pearl Harbor would be a surprise attack against our satellites in space (which have been used for military purposes since the first Iraq war). The attacks of 9/11 were obviously not that. But those attacks have definitely been seen as constituting the kind of new Pearl Harbor for which the authors of *Rebuilding America's Defenses* seemingly hoped. In fact, President Bush himself reportedly wrote in his diary on the night of 9/11: "The Pearl Harbor of the 21st century took place today."[81] Immediately after the attacks, in any case, both Henry Kissinger and *Time* magazine said that America should respond to the attacks of 9/11 in the same way it had responded to the attack on Pearl Harbor.[82]

The Attacks of 9/11 as "Opportunities"

Leading members of the Bush administration certainly regarded the attacks as providing opportunities. The word itself was, in fact, used several times. Donald Rumsfeld stated that 9/11 created "the kind of opportunities that World War II offered, to refashion the world." Condoleezza Rice told senior members of the National Security Council to "think about 'how do you capitalize on these opportunities' to fundamentally change . . . the shape of the world."[83] According to Bob Woodward, the president himself declared the attacks to have provided "a great opportunity."[84] This language even found its way into *NSS 2002*, which said: "The events of September 11, 2001 opened vast, new opportunities."[85]

These new opportunities enabled America's leaders to take another big step toward the completion of their drive to make America's non-accidental, non-benign empire truly global, with no borders.

The New American Militarism

In his 2003 book, *The Sorrows of Empire*, subtitled *Militarism, Secrecy, and the End of the Republic*, Chalmers Johnson said that the United States is "something other than what it professed to be"—that in reality it is "a military juggernaut intent on world domination."[86] At the end of *American Empire*, published in 2002, Andrew Bacevich suggested that the topic of "civil-military relations" was a dangerously neglected topic.[87] He then developed this theme in a 2005 book entitled *The New American Militarism*, in which he says that America has become a "military Leviathan."[88]

In using the adjective "new," Bacevich makes a twofold point. On the one hand, militarism did not suddenly develop under the Bush-Cheney administration. It has been a bipartisan project, which has been developing for some time, especially since the end of the Vietnam War. On the other hand, Bush and his advisors "have certainly taken up the mantle of this militarism with a verve."[89] At the heart of this enthusiasm is what Bacevich calls a marriage of "military metaphysics," meaning "a tendency to see international problems as military problems," with utopian expectations as to what can be achieved by military means.[90]

Besides greater enthusiasm for military adventures, this administration has added two new dimensions: "the Bush doctrine of preventive war," which Bacevich calls "the clearest articulation of the new American militarism,"[91] and the closely related idea that it is perfectly acceptable to use military force to bring about "regime change" in other countries.

While referring to the idea of preventive war as a "Bush doctrine," Bacevich knows that neither this idea nor that of regime change originated in the mind of George W. Bush. These doctrines were, rather, products of the neoconservative movement, which "laid the intellectual foundation of the new American militarism."[92]

A central part of laying this foundation has been the concerted effort to get Americans to accept and even take pride in the fact that their country is an imperial power. The statements by Krauthammer and others quoted earlier followed on a suggestion made some years earlier by Irving Kristol, one of the founders of the neoconservative movement. In 1986, with the end of the Cold War on the horizon, Kristol said that the United States needed to move toward a foreign policy of "global unilateralism." He said that it would be difficult to get most fellow Americans to accept this policy, however, because "we are an imperial power with no imperial self-definition."[93] One of the central goals of "neocons"—as members of the movement are often called—was to instill this new self-definition.

The foundation for the doctrine of preventive war in particular was laid by what Bacevich calls "second-generation neoconservative thinking,"[94] in which leading roles have been played by several thinkers quoted earlier, including Robert Kagan, Lawrence Kaplan, Charles Krauthammer, William Kristol, and Richard Perle. For these neocons, the United States should, in Kagan's 1996 words, "use [its military strength] actively to maintain a world order which both supports and rests upon American hegemony."[95]

From this neocon perspective, Bacevich says, the purpose of the Department of Defense is not primarily to defend and to deter, but "to transform the international order by transforming its constituent parts." The United States had not been able to use war for this purpose earlier because "the proximate threat posed by the Soviet Union had obliged the United States to exercise a certain self-restraint," but once this threat was gone, "the need for self-restraint fell away."[96]

In Bacevich's eyes, as this statement shows, these thinkers had never favored U.S. self-restraint on the basis of international law and morality. They had merely tolerated it as long as prudence demanded it. But once the bipolar world became unipolar, with only one superpower, they believed that America should use its power, without self-restraint, to achieve its interests.

Bacevich points out, moreover, that the present policy of the Department of Defense is in line with the advice of the neocons: Its primary mission now is "global power projection," with "defense per se figur[ing] as little more than an afterthought."[97]

The conclusion that the end of the Cold War led U.S. leaders to use military forces primarily for power projection is, Bacevich points out, supported by relative numbers. "During the entire Cold War era, from 1945 through 1988, large-scale U.S. military actions abroad totaled a scant six," but from the fall of the Berlin Wall in 1989 to the attack on Iraq in 2003, there were nine such actions. We went, in other words, from six in forty-eight years to nine in fourteen years! Speaking as a military man himself, Bacevich observes that "the tempo of U.S. military interventionism has become nothing short of frenetic."[98]

To be capable of using its strength in this proactive, transformative way, the U.S. military needs massive funding. The need for ever higher levels of military spending, accordingly, is a central—perhaps *the* central—theme of the neocons. It is certainly the central theme of *Rebuilding America's Defenses*, produced by the Project for the New American Century—a thoroughly neocon organization (chaired by Irvin Kristol's son William Kristol, founder of the *Weekly Standard*, which has become the main organ of neocon thinking). Moreover, Bacevich says, "[a]lthough the aftermath of 9/11 saw a quantum increase in U.S. defense spending, neocons lobbied for still more, . . . arguing for a permanent increase of $70 to $100 billion."[99]

The extent to which this attitude reflects an extremely militaristic outlook becomes even clearer when we consider the fact that, according to one calculation, "the United States spends more on defense than all other nations in the world together." According to that calculation, based on CIA data, the United States spends $380 billion annually on its military, hence over half of the world's total of $750 billion. Having cited this study, which was published in 2003, Bacevich comments, "If anything, that comparison understates the level of total U.S. spending."[100]

Indeed, according to a more recent study, that figure of $380 billion, as well as the official figure of $436.4 billion for 2004, grossly understates the amount of the U.S. budget devoted to military-related matters. Economics professor Jurgen Brauer, arguing against the "common misconception that U.S. defense expenditure is equivalent to the Department of Defense outlays," says that those official figures are very misleading. The Bureau of Economic Analysis (BEA), by including various military-related items, such as expenditures for nuclear weapons, that are not included in the budget for the Department of Defense, calculated that the outlay for military spending in 2004 was $548 billion. And Brauer's own calculations, which include interest payments on the portion of the national debt for which military spending is responsible, produced an even higher total, $765.6 billion, which is "75 percent more than the Department of Defense outlays." But whether one accepts the BEA figure or Brauer's, the generally accepted idea, that the government spends 19 cents of every tax dollar for defense compared with 81 cents for everything else, is extremely misleading. "The split really is 68 cents versus 32 cents. Defense is not one-fifth of federal spending but two-thirds of it."[101]

We have it on good authority that "where your treasure is, there will your heart be also" (Matt. 6:21). In light of the above figures—according to which the United States, even by a conservative estimate, already spends more for military purposes than all other nations combined, and according to which, by a more realistic estimate, more than two-thirds of our budget is devoted to military purposes (leaving less than one-third for health, education, welfare, the environment, and everything else)—we as a nation now have an *extremely* militaristic heart.

And yet the neocons, who now largely guide policy in Washington, want us to spend still more of our tax dollars on the military. If recent history is any guide, moreover, they will get their way.

At the end of a chapter devoted to the contribution made to the new American militarism by evangelical Christianity, Bacevich says, "Were it not for the support offered by several tens of millions of evangelicals, militarism in this deeply and genuinely religious country becomes inconceivable."[102] It is time for people of faith to realize that our country is not in the hands of other people of faith. It is in the hands of people of greed, served by fanatics animated by militaristic imperialism.

9/11 and the American Empire

I will conclude this chapter by discussing explicitly a topic only hinted at earlier: the question of responsibility for the attacks of 9/11. These terrorist attacks, as we have seen (and will continue to see throughout the volume), have been used as the basis for the extremely militaristic foreign policy of the Bush-Cheney administration under the guise of a "war on terror." And yet there is abundant evidence that the terrorist attacks of 9/11 were orchestrated by the Bush administration itself.

Many Americans are inclined, of course, to dismiss this idea out of hand on the grounds that they reject all "conspiracy theories." However, the official story about 9/11 is itself a conspiracy theory, according to which the attacks were planned and carried out entirely by members of al-Qaeda under the influence of Osama bin Laden. The question, accordingly, is not *whether* we accept a conspiracy theory about 9/11 but only *which one*—the conspiracy theory promulgated by the Bush-Cheney administration or the alternative theory, according to which the attacks were planned, or at least deliberately allowed, by this administration itself. The only rational way to decide between these two theories is to examine the relevant evidence.

And although I myself was at first doubtful that the evidence would be convincing, I found, once I actually began examining it, that it is extremely strong. In 2003, therefore, I wrote a book, *The New Pearl Harbor: Disturbing Questions about the Bush Administration and 9/11*, in which I summarized the evidence that had been discovered by previous researchers. This evidence, I said, provided a "strong *prima facie* case for official complicity."[103] Whether a *prima facie* case turns out to be *conclusive*, of course, depends on whether the evidence and arguments, when examined, turn out to be convincing.

In a criminal trial, once a *prima facie* case has been made, it is up to the defense attorney to rebut the various elements contained in the prosecution's evidence-based argumentation. This role could have been played by the 9/11 Commission. One might assume, to be sure, that it was to assume the stance of the disinterested judge or jury, simply evaluating the evidence presented to it—evidence supportive of the Bush administration's conspiracy theory, as well as evidence supportive of the alternative theory. The Commission's investigative work, however, was carried out by its staff, which was directed by Philip Zelikow,[104] and he was virtually a member of the Bush administration.[105]

Under Zelikow's leadership, therefore, the Commission took the role of the prosecuting attorney for the Bush administration's case against Osama bin Laden and al-Qaeda. In doing so, it implicitly played the role of the defense attorney for the Bush administration. A most important question to ask about *The 9/11 Commission Report*, therefore, is how well it rebutted the *prima facie* case against the Bush-Cheney administration.

The answer, as I showed in a second book, *The 9/11 Commission Report: Omissions and Distortions*, is that it simply ignored most of the evidence and distorted the rest. I cannot here summarize the various kinds of evidence that the Commission failed to rebut. But I can give a few examples.

The New Pearl Harbor (NPH) reported evidence that some of the alleged hijackers, all of whom were supposed to have died in the crashes, are still alive. But *The 9/11 Commission Report*, far from rebutting this evidence, fails even to mention it.[106]

NPH presented evidence that although Mohamed Atta, supposedly the ringleader of the hijackers, had been portrayed as a devout Muslim ready to meet his maker, he in reality loved alcohol, pork, prostitutes, and lap dances. However, the *Report*, claiming that Atta had become very religious, even "fanatically so," simply ignored all evidence to the contrary.[107]

NPH pointed out that the collapses of the Twin Towers and Building 7 of the World Trade Center had at least ten characteristics in common with controlled demolitions, in which buildings are brought down by explosives. But the *Report* fails to mention this fact or explain an alternative way in which those features could have been produced.[108]

NPH pointed out that the collapse of Building 7, which was not hit by an airplane, is especially hard to explain without referring to explosives, because steel-frame high-rise buildings have never—before 9/11 or afterwards—been caused to collapse by fire alone. The *Report*, however, avoided discussing this most difficult problem by simply not mentioning that Building 7 collapsed.[109]

NPH pointed out that if the official "pancake" theory of the collapses of Twin Towers were true, the 47 massive steel columns that constituted the core of each tower would have still been sticking up several hundred feet in the air. The *Report*, however, avoided explaining why they were not still standing by claiming that the core of each tower consisted of "a hollow steel shaft."[110]

NPH pointed out many reasons to conclude that the Pentagon was *not* struck by Flight 77. The *Report*, however, fails to rebut or even mention any of this evidence.[111]

NPH reported evidence that in July 2001, when Osama bin Laden was already America's "most wanted" criminal, he was treated by an American doctor in the American Hospital in Dubai and visited by the local CIA agent. NPH also reported evidence that *after* 9/11, the US military in Afghanistan deliberately let bin Laden escape. The *Report*, however, fails to discuss any of this evidence.[112]

NPH presented many types of evidence that Flight 93 was shot down by the US military. But the *Report* failed to deal with any of this evidence.[113]

This is only a small sample of the omissions and distortions contained in *The 9/11 Commission Report*. My study, in fact, documented 115 omissions and distortions.[114] This sample is sufficient, however, to illustrate how egregiously the 9/11 Commission failed to answer the *prima facie* case for the claim that the Bush administration was itself responsible for 9/11.

In a criminal trial, it is the responsibility of the defense attorneys, once the *prima facie* case has been made, to rebut the various kinds of evidence presented by the prosecuting attorneys. If they fail to do this, then the *prima facie* case is deemed by the judge or the jury to be *conclusive*. The 9/11 Commission had the opportunity to rebut the *prima facie* case against the Bush administration but failed to do so. It would not be unreasonable, therefore, to conclude that the *prima facie* case can now be considered a conclusive case.

Readers will, to be sure, want to examine the evidence for themselves before drawing this inference. But if after examining this evidence they conclude that there is indeed a strong *prima facie* case for the Bush administration's guilt and that the 9/11 Commission did indeed fail to respond to this evidence, then it would be reasonable for them to conclude that members of the Bush-Cheney administration were behind the 9/11 attacks. This would be reasonable, at least, if they could see that this administration would have had a sufficient motive.

However, we need only look at the benefits the administration reaped from 9/11 to see *several* plausible motives: they wanted a huge increase in military spending, which, they knew, would be forthcoming after "a new Pearl Harbor"; they wanted a climate, consisting of fear and desires for revenge, in which Americans would support a "war on terror" that could be used as a cover for enlarging the empire; they wanted a pretext to carry out the pre-planned wars to bring about regime change in Afghanistan and Iraq; and they wanted, more generally, a climate in which Americans would accept the new doctrines of preventive war and regime change.

Seeing that the Bush-Cheney White House would have had abundant motives for arranging the attacks of 9/11 strengthens, of course, the reasons for concluding that it did just that. As Bacevich himself says (albeit without himself implying official complicity in the attacks), "the events of 9/11 provided the tailor-made opportunity to break free of the fetters restricting the exercise of American power."[115]

If we conclude that the Bush-Cheney White House, in collusion with Pentagon leaders, did orchestrate the attacks of 9/11, then the implications for our attitude toward the American empire are enormous. This conclusion would add another powerful piece of evidence that America's global domination project cannot be considered benign. In fact, as I have written elsewhere, this conclusion would help us *"fully* grasp the extent to which this project is propelled by fanaticism based on a deeply perverted value system."[116]

In chapter 6, I will suggest how the present world order, dominated by this value system, could be replaced with a democratic world order, in which the basic values of Christianity, Judaism, Islam, and the other world religions might play a much greater role.

Chapter 2

Imperialism in American Economic Policy

John B. Cobb Jr.

For twenty years or more, I have been concerned about the global economy and with trying to show the way in which economic theory has become the basic theology of the world. I have been working to undercut the commitment to that theory as a basis for overall social, political, and economic policy. There are problems with economic theory even within the narrow province in which it is properly used, but my main complaint is that it has been extended far beyond that limited province, so that the rest of our social lives have been subordinated to the goals toward which economic theory is directed.[1]

In other words, instead of having the economy embedded in the society, which in turn is embedded in the wider ecological context, we have made the economy the overall context. Education is for the sake of the economy, government is for the sake of the economy, and sometimes religion is for the sake of the economy.

Because economic theory has become the dominant ideology for the whole culture, it is very important to ask whether its assumptions are adequate and correct. If, as I believe, the answer is negative, it seems urgent to remove from the policies that follow from economic theory the aura of moral justification that they have assumed and have persuaded many people to accept.

Removing moral authority from these policies will not end them. But what distresses me most is that so many people of goodwill, including so many Christians, have accepted the idea that the way forward for society as a whole is based on an economic theory that has no place for community, no place for justice, and no place for the natural world. Policies based on that theory have been immensely destructive for human communities everywhere, have led to extremely unjust distribution of goods, and have extensively degraded the natural world.

I recognize the importance of power. I do not suppose that undercutting the ring of truth and morality about the dominant global policies will lead to their

23

sudden collapse. But it should at least weaken the support that has been given these policies by those who are genuinely people of goodwill, concerned about overcoming poverty in the world. These policies are supported by transnational corporations, governments, and the elites who benefit from them. In short, they have behind them the power of the global economic and political establishment.

Nevertheless, moral support has also been important. It should prove useful, therefore, to drive a wedge between those who act out of simple self-interest and those who are morally committed to the currently dominant policies because of the illusion that they are justified by the best available theory. This separation is in fact happening to some extent, as more people of goodwill have joined the protests against the dominant global policies that follow from the wooden application of neoliberal economic theory.

In the past few years, the issue of the American empire has emerged as an even more urgent concern. Terms such as "global dominance," "global hegemony," and "*Pax Americana*," now widely used, all point to imperialist policies of the United States. Since many supporters of these policies now accept and use the term "empire," the discussion can proceed on this basis without concern to avoid supposedly inflammatory terminology. The issue is whether the military, political, and economic domination of the world by one superpower is desirable.

Believing, as I do, that the economy is immensely important, I will continue to focus on economic developments. But my way of looking at these developments is changing. I will not treat them simply as the working out by conscientious people of the implications of a particular theory. I will emphasize instead the ways in which economic policies have become a useful tool through which American imperialism has operated. John Perkins, an insider to these practices, has helped us recognize this and understand it better. In *Confessions of an Economic Hit Man*, he has explained how the United States has for decades used deceptive development loans to make the borrowing nations permanently subservient.[2] Viewing recent history in political terms does not lead to rejection of what can be said when economic issues are in focus, but the picture that emerges is different.

I am indebted to the administration of George W. Bush for this shift in my perceptions. I am not alone in having come to understand better what our country has been doing for a long time because of the directness with which the neoconservatives express and advocate the deeper, long-practiced, but often obscured and denied, goals of American foreign policy. Our historic behavior is no longer mysterious. We no longer have to grope around to find the hidden purposes of American international behavior. These purposes are no longer hidden. Once we recognize the role of imperialism in American policy for what it has been and continues to be, we can trace it back to the beginnings of European exploration and settlement of the New World. This chapter, however, will concentrate on the period since the Second World War.

The Creation of the Bretton Woods Institutions

At the end of World War II, two types of international institutions were created. One type was political, with the United Nations as its chief example. The other type was economic, with the chief examples being the Bretton Woods institutions. From the beginning, the United States made clear that it planned to play the dominant role in all of these organizations.

In the United Nations, the United States determined that it would not be just one of the five powers with veto, but the most important of these. The economic lever was one very important instrument of control. Nevertheless, the U.S. participation in the United Nations expressed more than sheer American imperialism. It expressed a view that it would be possible to have an improved international order over against the one that had been present before World War II. It expressed some regret on the part of Americans that they had rejected the League of Nations, with some recognition that this was a mistake and may have contributed to the events that led up to World War II. There was some passion for working with others for peace and justice, some genuine idealism mixed with narrow national self-interest and desire for imperial control. Despite the intended and realized dominance of the United States in the United Nations, the American participation in the establishment of that organization was not simply an imperialistic move.

The self-interest of the United States was more blatant in the creation of the Bretton Woods institutions. It was clear that the International Monetary Fund and the World Bank would be located in Washington, D.C. It was clear that the United States would have by far the loudest and strongest voice, and that Americans would normally head both institutions. American dominance was not a question.

At that point, except for the Communist sphere, most of the world, prostrated as it was by the war, was not unhappy that the United States assumed leadership. Outside the Western Hemisphere, the United States was not viewed as an imperialist threat. In general, it did not have to cram the new world order down reluctant throats.

One element in the American program did point clearly in the direction of American imperial interests. In this case, the interests were commercial, rather than military or political. The Bretton Woods conference was an occasion for ending the self-enclosedness of the British Empire. The United States made it very clear that Britain would no longer be able to have an empire within which it could control trade and investments. The United States wanted access to that empire and, of course, got it. This could be seen as a contribution to the breaking up of the British Empire and, accordingly, as a contra-imperialist move. The idea was that the countries composing that empire would be treated just like all other countries and not have special economic relationships with Great Britain. Hence, although we can now see how this contributed to American economic imperialism, at the time it did not seem imperialist to most of the world.

The American people were ready for multilateral, global activity, with the United States as first among equals—maybe first without any equals—but with, nevertheless, some respect for the autonomy, or at least the voices, of other people. Just as the United Nations came into being partly because people did not want to go through another world war, the Bretton Woods institutions came into being because people did not want to go through another depression. Of course, this suited American interests. On this matter, however, American interests and those of many other people in the world tended to converge; so the issue of motive did not seem important. That nations act in their own interest was largely assumed. The question was more whether their interests were enlightened, worked together with others' interests, and took long-term consequences into account.

The war encouraged the needed long-term thinking. Many commentators have written about the domination of thought and policy today by the anticipated bottom line only six months later. Politicians also plan, typically, for the very short term. At the end of a terrible war, on the other hand, many people wanted to think about the next generation and not just the next year or two. This had some effect on what went on in both San Francisco and Bretton Woods. At the time, it was the founding of the United Nations in San Francisco that generated excitement. Relatively few people paid attention to what went on at Bretton Woods; it seemed very technical, very obscure. And perhaps for some years the United Nations was in fact more important.

But later, the United States shifted power from the United Nations to the two Bretton Woods institutions—the International Monetary Fund (IMF) and the World Bank. They have become by far the more potent determinants of what goes on in the world. And, for the most part, they function as tools of American policy.

From 1945 to 1980

During the postwar period to 1980, the imperial thrust, although detectable in many different places, continued to be checked and muted. This was due chiefly to the Cold War. The United States did not want to be the only country in the world opposing the Soviet Union. It wanted most of the rest of the world to be on its side. Its policies needed to build a large coalition to oppose the Soviet Union as a military power, and also to oppose communism as an ideology and a form of government.

Communist states and Communist parties normally allied themselves with the Soviet Union. Accordingly, to reduce the attraction of communism to American and other workers, the American elite allowed the implementation of policies generally favorable to industrial workers. Hence the New Deal continued to operate and expand in American society. Indeed, there was, internal to the United States, considerable power sharing. As a result, U.S. unions did quite well during this period, labor was rather powerful, wages rose, and the nation implemented a structure of taxation that taxed the rich more heavily than the poor. The nation moved, although not nearly as much as the European nations, in the direction of guaranteeing minimum support to all its citizens.

These policies were successful in preventing sympathy for Marxism from gaining a significant foothold within this country. The great majority of Americans felt that the American system was giving them increasing opportunities to participate in the economy and its affluence. They were not interested in considering a different system. The sacrifices required to contain the Soviet Union were willingly accepted.

The American economic elite grudgingly allowed these liberal policies to prevail during this period because of the Cold War. That the Cold War was the reason for this toleration is shown by the speed with which things changed when the Soviet threat diminished. In the next section, we will see that the direction taken by successive American administrations since 1980 has been dramatically different.

During those first decades after World War II, the American people to some extent acted on an American idealistic self-understanding. Support for the Marshall Plan illustrates this. Of course, the Marshall Plan was also part of Cold War strategy. If western Europe had remained in a miserable condition for twenty years, it probably would have gone communist, and that would have shifted the balance of power to the Soviet Union. Further, the Marshall Plan benefited some important economic groups in the United States, without whose support it would not have been enacted. Nevertheless, the sustained support of the Marshall Plan required the general goodwill of Americans toward the people of Europe.

Humanitarian concerns and Cold War policies also both played major roles with respect to policies toward the third world. The rhetoric of our country, seeking to capture humanitarian sentiments, expressed real interest in third-world development. Certain actions accorded somewhat with this rhetoric. However, the primary reason for devoting resources to development stemmed from the Cold War. The effort was to keep as many third-world countries as possible on the American side of that war, and keeping them there required that many people in those countries see some promise of improvement by siding with the United States. Sadly, as time passed, humanitarian concerns played a decreasing role.

The general policy was that each of the third-world countries could decide, with the help of World Bank advisors and others, how to go about developing. The usual model was that of national economies engaged in international trade, but nevertheless able to make the basic decisions about how to order their own internal affairs and their own internal economy. Some countries did very well with this system; others did not do well at all. There was a kind of double development. On the one hand, in spite of the fact that the United States would grant and lend money, and the World Bank and other banks would invest in various projects, the development that took place in most countries benefited only the elites in those countries and in the lending countries, not the masses of people.

Some of this was quite contrary to the intentions of the World Bank. Many of the people in the bank, including Robert McNamara, really did want to reduce poverty. They said they did, and sometimes they engaged in massive efforts to do so. But trying to reduce poverty by building dams—and that was the World Bank's favorite mode of development—creates a lot of poverty. On the one hand, the elites who control the water and the electricity became richer. On the other hand, poor people, who had survived by farming or fishing, had their livelihoods destroyed. The unintended consequence was that the gap between the poor and the rich in third-world countries grew.

Because the most important political goal of the U.S. leaders was to have the support of the elites in the third world, this maldistribution was not deeply distressing. The elites determined which side of the Cold War their countries would be on and whether the goods that they produced would be denied to the Soviet bloc while being made available to the United States and its allies.

The poor were getting poorer, but this did not bother those in our government whom we now call the imperialists. The primary goal of aid was achieved as long as the elites were satisfied with the type of development that was taking place in their countries. Hence, the United States was willing to invest, to lend, and even to give, in order to make that development possible.

However, even the elites in the third world were not fully satisfied. They felt that the terms of trade, which probably made more difference in their economies than the gifts and loans from first-world countries and international banks, were more and more destructive to their economies. Third-world countries mostly produced commodities, while they had to import machinery and other high-tech goods. The price of what they imported went up, and the price of what they exported went down. Even if the elites were doing relatively well, they saw that their nations were losing ground in relation to the first world.

Accordingly, an important effort in this period, especially in the 1970s, was the attempt of third-world governments to work together to create an alternative voice. This voice did not support the first world against the second world or the second world against the first world. Instead it declared a plague on both those houses. It called for a New Economic Order in which the terms of trade would favor their goods instead of exploiting them. This new order would make it possible for third-world nations to engage in their own economic development.

This new voice was being heard quite effectively within the United Nations General Assembly. Some of the organizations of the United Nations were sympathetic to it. It seemed to be gaining influence, so it could not be ignored.

The third-world voice became still stronger with the rise of the Organization of Petroleum Exporting Countries. This was the one great political and economic success of the New Economic Order. By working together, the oil-producing countries could set the price of oil to their own advantage without asking the United States, western Europe, or Japan their opinion.

This development was a threat to U.S. hegemony and to the economies of Europe and Japan as well. The United States feared that the success of OPEC would inspire other groups of third-world nations to form cartels around the commodities the industrial nations needed to import from them. In this way, the third world, instead of being obviously weak and a pawn in the hands of the United States, would become itself a powerful economic player on the world scene.[3]

The Reagan Years and Neoliberal Economics

During the 1970s, these matters came to a head, and in 1980 Ronald Reagan came to office with the determination to ensure that U.S. hegemony would not be threatened. Setting the price of oil without our permission was an act of rebellion that could not be tolerated. So, in a way, Ronald Reagan declared war on the third world. This war took a number of directions.

One tactic was to undercut the power of the United Nations. Reagan worked at that systematically, transferring all economic thinking and decision making to the World Bank and the IMF, which could be much more successfully controlled by the Treasury Department of the United States.

A second tactic was for the United States simply to refuse to pay its contribution to the United Nations until the latter made some demanded changes. Through this means, America was able to demonstrate its enormous power over the United Nations. Reagan's hand may have been strengthened by the fact that the United Nations was already viewed with great suspicion by conservatives in this country. In any case, Reagan punished the United Nations for allowing strong voices not supportive of the United States to play a role.

The Third-World Debt Crisis

A third tactic involved the third-world debt crisis, which came to a head shortly after Reagan came into office. Explaining this tactic will require a brief history.

The problem of third-world debt is the cumulative result of the post–World War II policy of encouraging development by borrowing. The theory was that third-world countries could invest borrowed money efficiently and pay it back from the proceeds, while accumulating industrial plant and infrastructure. To this day, this plan has rarely worked. The interest on debt has generally been repaid not from profits but by denying services to the poor and by borrowing more money more often. Some of these effects have resulted from the cynical deceit that Perkins has shown to have been an instrument of U.S. policy. Some of it resulted from deflecting money that could have been used for profitable investments into military and other noncommercial purposes and into the Swiss bank accounts of corrupt rulers. These are problems that have continued and grown worse as the debt has continued to increase to the present.[4]

The crisis in 1980 was due to the added problems caused by OPEC.

The Mexican Crisis and Structural Adjustment

In the case of Mexico, the crisis was the result of the fact that OPEC dollars were being loaned at very favorable terms to third-world governments. Mexico had borrowed a lot of this money—some of it being well used, much of it used corruptly. Often these loans were at an interest rate that was lower than the level of inflation. It is hard to refuse money when it is offered that way. Then, toward the end of the decade, interest rates rose very rapidly, and Mexico could not keep up with its debt. It threatened to declare bankruptcy. This was a crisis for the commercial banks that had loaned it money as well as for Mexico.

This crisis provided a marvelous opportunity to the Reagan administration. Mexico's government and the Mexican elite were persuaded that bankruptcy was not an acceptable solution, so they cooperated with the IMF and the World Bank to prevent it. These institutions brought creditors together, renegotiated everything, and created a situation in which Mexico could survive without going bankrupt. This plan was a great success.

What did Mexico have to do in order to gain these concessions from creditors? It had to accept "structural adjustment." Structural adjustment was an idea that developed in the World Bank under Robert McNamara. The World Bank, puzzled that pouring money into countries produced few benefits, decided to track this money. It found out that structural problems in the society kept the money from being well invested. These structures kept the money in the hands of the elite and out of the hands of the poor. The original idea behind structural adjustment loans was that they would help the country change its basic structures, thereby enabling it to become more effective in the use of its money. This would have been a moderate and reasonable approach for dealing with a serious problem.

However, the structural adjustment imposed on Mexico in 1982 actually functioned in a very different way. Prior to 1982, Mexico aimed at a national economy. Structural adjustment forced it to abandon this pattern and integrate its economy into the emerging global economy. Instead of developing structures that would enable the poor to benefit from development, the new pattern actually exacerbated the gap between the rich and the poor.

When the Mexican government, prior to 1982, was still committed to a national economy, it aimed to strengthen the economy of Mexico, keeping it in Mexican hands. In theory, and to some extent in practice, this meant improving the economic condition of all Mexicans, including the poor, by its own internal Mexican policies. Mexico aimed to keep national ownership of its oil. The government, besides owning many businesses itself, required that majority ownership of all firms remain in the hands of Mexicans. It maintained agricultural policies that had been put in place for the sake of the peasants. It protected both Mexican industries and Mexican peasants by tariffs. There were many problems and much inefficiency and corruption, but there had also been considerable economic progress since World War II.

However, from 1982 forward, the national economy was systematically dismantled. A different ideal prevailed. This ideal followed from neoliberal economic theory, which prizes private ownership and free competition above all else. Government-owned business should be privatized, and government should play the smallest possible role in regulating private business. All economic resources in the country should be as available for purchase and control by foreigners as by citizens. Producers in one locale should compete with producers everywhere else in the world. Nothing should be subsidized or protected. The ideal is a laissez-faire global market in which each region specializes in what it can produce most efficiently and imports what can be produced more efficiently elsewhere.

Structural adjustment was designed to move Mexico toward this radically different ideal. Of course, the shift could not be made all at once. But beginning in 1982, Mexico has come a long way toward integration into the global economy. It made many concessions at that time, made more concessions with the North American Free Trade Agreement, and more still in the years since then. Instead of aiming at Mexican control of Mexican business, it adopts policies that will attract foreign investment. Mexico sets wages, not to promote the well-being of workers, but for the sake of competing with other third-world countries for new factories built by transnational corporations. Mexico no longer develops environmental policies for the long-term well-being of its people, but in order to attract foreign investors. In short, Mexico no longer controls its own economy. What happens economically in Mexico today is determined more by decisions made by transnational corporations, the U.S. government, the IMF, the World Bank, and the World Trade Organization (WTO) than by decisions made in Mexico City.

No government can be indifferent to the economy in which its people are immersed. Washington largely speaks for the transnational corporations, dominates the other institutions that control the Mexican economy, and is also of great importance in its direct actions. Accordingly, the Mexican government is necessarily subservient to it.

Structural Adjustment for All

The approach taken to the Mexican debt crisis was then applied to other debtor nations. Structural adjustment has transformed the world's economy. Its importance both economically and politically has not yet been fully appreciated.

Much of the hardship brought about by structural adjustment resulted from the model developed in 1982, which was designed to enable Mexico to pay its debts. To do so, Mexico had to export more than it imported, so that the government would have revenues larger than its expenditures. Since import duties were discouraged, structural adjustment required lowering the income of consumers, with the result that they could not buy imported goods. Reducing purchasing power was usually achieved by depreciating the currency without increasing wages. Currency depreciation makes exports cheaper and imports more expensive. It also creates great hardship, especially among those who were already poor.

The Level Playing Field and Double Standards

One other feature of structural adjustment and the global economy should be noted. The theory that justifies structural adjustment calls for a "level playing field" within the global economy. That would mean that the rich nations adopt the same rules they impose on the poor ones. But in fact they have not done so. For example, Europe and the United States continue to subsidize their agricultural producers heavily. This practice makes their surplus production cheap on the world market. Peasants in poor countries have to compete, without subsidies or tariff protection, with highly subsidized American agribusiness.

The United States sometimes claims that the lower prices of our products are due to the superiority of American farmers, but this claim has no basis in fact. It has been calculated that the total subsidies to agriculture in this country and the total profits from agriculture are about the same. So there is no profit from actually producing the food at current market prices. The profit comes simply from the contributions of U.S. taxpayers. It is not politically possible for the U.S. government to end subsidies to American agriculture, since these go mainly to very powerful transnational corporations.

One of the stories that I find most painful is about Haiti. Because Haiti is in the Western Hemisphere, any resistance by Haitians to the hegemony of the United States has been peculiarly resented. We systematically undercut any effort by democratically elected governments there to act on behalf of the needs of their own people. Accordingly, the Haitian government was forced to give up its subsidies to the rice farmers. Then the United States exported heavily subsidized rice from the San Francisco area at a price below what it costs the unsubsidized Haitian farmers to produce it. In a country where the majority of the people are farmers, the economic consequences have been disastrous.

This is a clear case in which policy was determined by imperial interests, closely connected with U.S. commercial interests, rather than by the professed goal, supported by neoliberal economic theory, of implementing a level playing field. Such policies, while applying the requirements of economic theory to third-world nations in a way that disempowers them, exempts the first world from these requirements, thereby strengthening American control of the market everywhere. This historic reality has created resentment and resistance even among third-world elites who have otherwise bought into the ideal of the global market.

The Effects of Structural Adjustment

Regardless of what the poor in third-world countries might have gained from structural adjustment as originally conceived, the result of the structural adjustment actually imposed upon them has been disastrous. In Mexico peasants have lost their land and been forced to move to urban slums, to enter the United States illegally, or to work in the maquiladoras along the border. Meanwhile, real wages have declined and resistance by labor to exploitation by transnational corporations has been suppressed. On the other hand, the number of Mexican billionaires has increased dramatically.

In much of the world, furthermore, the pace of economic growth that structural adjustment was supposed to accelerate has slowed or even been reversed. The third world has been reorganized for the sake of increasing subservience to Washington and for repayment of debts to the first world. This has not occurred without resistance, but this resistance did not begin with structural adjustment. In Latin America, peasant resistance to exploitation is much older. The United States has intervened repeatedly, sometimes directly with its own troops, sometimes through local military forces, to prevent the overthrow of governments subservient to it by those concerned for the welfare of ordinary people. It has intervened even to reverse changes of government achieved by democratic elections.

Since World War II, the United States has trained troops from Latin American countries to suppress peasant restiveness. The School of the Americas at Fort Benning, Georgia, has specialized in teaching what is called low-intensity warfare, which includes torture. During the Cold War, opposition to oppressive governmental policies by workers and peasants was labeled "communist," thus providing an additional justification for suppression. But the end of the Cold War did not bring an end to the protests of the poor. The effects of structural adjustment have led to continued protests and uprisings. The School of the Americas continues its instruction, partly in Panama.

U.S. Policies in East Asia

The global economy has been brought into being partly by the selective application of neoliberal economic thinking under the Reagan administration. For the inclusive goal, however, it was not enough to force the third world to integrate itself into the U.S.-controlled global economy. Reagan also had to deal with East Asia. He was unhappy that national economies in East Asia had succeeded brilliantly. They had not developed under neoliberal policies at all, but with systems that involved very close relationships between the government and industrial leaders. I am not arguing that such relations are ideal. I am simply observing that this type of economic system, which was quite different from the kind Reagan wanted to promote, was more successful as measured by the widely touted norm of economic growth.

Furthermore, as long as there are national economies that do not depend primarily on decisions made elsewhere, either by transnational corporations or by the U.S. government, there is more potential for resistance to policies favored by Washington. Since the East Asian countries were not indebted, the standard means of destroying their economic independence by structural adjustment was not available.

Therefore it was important for the United States to undercut these national economies by some other means. This was done, first, by giving them a bad name. The term "crony capitalism" emerged at this time. These economies were not free from corruption, to be sure, but it is not clear that they were more corrupt than the U.S. economy. In any case, they worked better than the U.S. system and far better than the system the United States was imposing on countries around the world.

One must note that, to this date, not a single country has successfully developed on neoliberal principles. All successful development, at least in its early stages, has taken place on the principles of national economy. This is true of the United States, in which the Civil War was waged by the North partly to defend its tariffs against the South's preference for free trade. This is just as true in the case of the current great success story, China, as it was of Japan, South Korea, Taiwan, and Singapore.

The United States was not interested in the success of international development programs as measured by benefits to the poor. It was interested in making sure that no part of the world would be outside the global economy, which enriched the American elite and functioned as the instrument of U.S. control. In this, Reagan was far more successful in relation to the third world than in relation to East Asia. Of course, East Asian countries (especially those in the south) were subsequently pushed further into the global market, which in turn made them vulnerable to the financial crisis that developed in the mid-1990s. In general they suffered in proportion to their abandonment of control over their own finances. This crisis enabled foreign capital to buy up many businesses at fire-sale prices. As a result, those countries are even less able now to manage their own affairs.

The two countries least affected by the East Asian crisis were the ones that would not obey the World Bank and the IMF. Malaysia decided to adopt policies that would control its own currency, and it came through the crisis quite well. As punishment for this success, Malaysia has been given a bad name by the press—which seldom mentions the fact that the neoliberal policies pushed by the IMF and the World Bank consistently destabilize economies. The other country, China, has yet to come under IMF and World Bank control, and it has weathered the East Asian crisis without much difficulty.

The dominance of neoliberal economics has major consequences in relation to both the global economy and American imperialism. One such principle is free trade—a nice-sounding phrase. What it means, however, is that no country outside the first world can control its own economy. The destiny of each now depends on the global market. Therefore the market, which is controlled by others, especially the United States, is in control of their destinies.

Argentina

Whereas movement toward free trade weakened the East Asian economies, it *destroyed* the third-world economies. That term is not too strong in relation to much of Africa. However, the most extreme case is Argentina, where the paper economy collapsed almost completely. The reasons of course are complex, but the basic cause was Argentina's full acceptance of the neoliberal principles promoted by the IMF. Argentina had been the IMF poster child, because it not only did everything the IMF required, but even went beyond these requirements.

Europe

Whereas the application of neoliberal economic principles to the third world and then to East Asia has been very effective in reducing the independence of nations and peoples, Europe has retained most of its autonomy. Nevertheless, even Europe has been adversely affected. European nations had moved far in the direction of democratic socialism. They were not vulnerable to being structurally adjusted by the IMF and the World Bank. However, economic globalization has made it far more difficult for Europe to maintain the high level of welfare-state services that it had attained. Europe is now being forced to choose between high unemployment, on the one side, and lower wages and reduced benefits, on the other. The "reform" for which economists now call in Europe is designed to unravel the welfare state.

The U.S. Internal Economy

Much of this analysis also applies internally to the United States. By the time Reagan became president, there was no longer much danger of generating a

Marxist backlash to policies here. So one of the first things he did was to undermine labor unions. He did this quite directly. But more importantly, he did it indirectly. By making the U.S. economy part of the global economy, he made American workers compete with workers in third-world countries. Millions of well-paying jobs in the United States were exported to low-wage countries. Industrial labor unions, once the backbone of organized labor, were decimated. Industries that remained in the United States could control their workers by the threat of moving outside the country. Strong unions are possible now only among workers such as longshoremen, teachers, and government workers, that is, those with jobs that cannot be shipped out of the country.

Since 1980, partly for these reasons, while the Gross Domestic Product, corporate earnings, and CEO salaries have soared, people in the bottom half of the economy have actually lost ground. This is not an accident. The globalization of the economy was guaranteed to have that effect, which was the effect that was wanted. Reagan intended to undo the New Deal, and he made a significant beginning.

That project has been continued by the Republican Party since then and has been intensified by the Bush-Cheney administration. The main feature of the New Deal that Reagan did not dare to attack was Social Security. This too has now come under siege.

To complete this program of global domination and reversal of the New Deal, the United States needs to have a society that is more fully controlled by the economic elite than was the case prior to the Reagan administration. Our new leadership has been working in that direction very successfully.

Other Developments

If the imperial project is to be fully successful, competing centers of power have to be eliminated. Reagan's policies undercut resistance by third-world governments. As these policies continue to work their way out, they are more slowly undermining the strength of East Asian and European powers. The next step had to do with the Soviet Union itself. That empire imploded. Many of the reasons had to do with internal developments little influenced by U.S. policies. But Reagan's acceleration of the arms race probably contributed.

The Success of the Reagan Revolution

Some may question the sequence here, but we should acknowledge the brilliance of the Reagan administration. If we measure the greatness of a presidency by the effective changes made both in the nation and in the world,

Reagan has been our greatest president. I intensely dislike the directions he moved us, but the Reagan administration changed the course of history more dramatically than did any previous one.

Successor administrations have not seriously tried to reverse the changes that Reagan instituted. They may slow them down or moderate them in some ways. But it is not just the Republican Party that is implementing the Reagan revolution. Both parties carry it forward. Both parties join in the pursuit of empire. Both support policies and actions directed to controlling the world, largely through economic means, but always with the threat of military force where there is resistance. Since the end of the Cold War, these policies have proven extremely successful.

Multilateral vs. Unilateral Imperialism

The main issue among the American elite has been the extent to which we implement our imperial ambitions unilaterally, compared with the extent to which we make use of multilateral organizations. Obviously the use of multilateral organizations obscures, and somewhat moderates, the imperial character of what is being done. The shift of the Bush-Cheney administration to blatantly unilateral action has awakened many of us to the deeper imperial policy of our nation.

The Clinton administration strongly supported the imperial direction of American policy through implementing the North American Free Trade Agreement and strengthening the World Trade Organization. Clinton also vigorously promoted the Free Trade Agreement of the Americas. He thus pushed for the globalization of the economy as strongly as had Reagan.

Nevertheless, there was a difference. Clinton pushed programs that had a multilateral character, at least in appearance. He sought agreements among countries and then supported international institutions to implement them. Or he used the international institutions to generate agreements. Although Clinton would not have hesitated to engage in unilateral action when needed, he preferred to accomplish American imperial goals through multilateral arrangements.

Reagan himself was mixed on this issue. His success in greatly weakening the United Nations made it possible thereafter for the United States to return to operate within it and largely determine its direction. The first President Bush's success in getting the United Nations to support the first Gulf War was an example of how that organization could be used by our government to cover and implement its policies.

The history of the World Trade Organization (WTO) is particularly interesting in this respect. Some at the Bretton Woods conference thought that, in addition to creating the World Bank and the IMF, the meeting should also produce an international trade organization. At that time, however, the United States thought it would do better by handling matters on a bilateral basis with respect to trade, rather than have an international organization that might set up rules that would inhibit American action. As time went by, the United States decided that it could achieve its hegemonic goals better through multinational agreements; so it pushed for these through several rounds of what were called General Agreements on Tariffs and Trade (GATT). More and more, America shifted from being opposed to an international trade organization to supporting one and pushing hard for its establishment. The WTO was the result. The WTO works to implement the same kind of policies as those imposed by structural adjustment.

However, beginning with the WTO meeting in Seattle in 1999, it has not been successful in pushing forward the U.S. agenda. Third-world countries have organized to demand more equal rules for first- and third-world countries. One way to read the events at the WTO meeting in Miami in 2003 is to suggest that the United States decided it was not worth making any significant concessions in order to keep the WTO going. If it cannot get its agenda accepted there, it may shift its efforts back to bilateral relationships with smaller, weaker countries. Dealing with them one by one, the United States can unilaterally press them into obedience and punish those that do not conform. It can thereby break through the limitation on American power that multilateral opposition can still achieve.

The increasing resistance to the proposals of the United States is the result not only of its unwillingness to play by the rules it forces on other nations but also of the extremes to which it is pushing liberalization and globalization. One example is the banking system. Since it is the banks that expand or contract the funds available for investment within a country, a government can have little influence on the fiscal health of a nation without some control over banking. But the United States is pushing third-world countries to open up their financial institutions to competition with transnational ones, whose vastly greater resources give them the advantage. Local banks are also to be available for purchase by foreigners.

The United States has also been committed to having agreements that would prevent countries from violating the patents of other countries, for example, with pharmaceuticals. If third-world countries must buy drugs from the United States, the prices are very high. The drug companies say this is because they spend a huge amount of money in drug development, and it is not worthwhile to develop new drugs unless they can profit from their production. While this argument is partly true, it is also misleading, since much of the cost of development of new drugs is borne by foundations and the government (that is, U.S. taxpayers).

But when people in third-world countries need drugs for life itself and they are not available at affordable prices, there is some resistance to this argument. This is especially true when the drugs can easily be manufactured locally and sold at a fraction of the U.S. price. Many are unwilling to see their people die in order that American pharmaceutical companies make large profits.

The Bush-Cheney Administration

Thus far, I have been reviewing the success of the Reagan administration and this country's subsequent political and economic moves that have proved so devastating to many third-world economies. Initially, it was not clear that the Bush-Cheney administration would act very differently on these matters than did the Clinton-Gore administration. Then the events of September 11, 2001, provided the occasion for issues—most of them discussed within our administration prior to that time—to be settled in a particular direction.

One of the necessities for an effective empire is the control of one's own people. Although the Reagan revolution had already impoverished a lot of people and concentrated wealth much more strongly in the hands of a small percentage of the population, it had not directly attacked our civil liberties in any massive way. There were people in the government before this time who certainly wanted to reduce our ability to protest government actions, since it is more difficult to build an empire abroad when there are massive protests at home against imperial policies. But the political situation was not then ripe for major changes.

However, the events of 9/11 made national security the primary issue, and individual rights can be curtailed in the name of security. Much of what is in the USA PATRIOT Act is more directed to providing a context in which civil disobedience and protest can be controlled than to preventing foreign nationals from attacking us. People can become frightened about engaging in protests because of the potential consequences of protests, or they may actually be severely punished if they do take part. This does not mean that the PATRIOT Act has nothing to do with real security, of course, but it has provided an opportunity to implement steps that make it easier for a U.S. administration to act without the support of its people.

The decision to act with or without the support of its people has been accompanied by the decision to act with or without the support of other nations. As long as international support is easily procured, the United States will work with others. If it is not readily available, the United States will act alone. We saw earlier that this policy is now affecting America's relation to the WTO. The appointment of Paul Wolfowitz to head the World Bank suggests that any qualification of its primary role as implementer of U.S. policy will no longer be tolerated. But the most important shift has been elsewhere.

September 11 also provided the occasion for deciding that unilateral action would supersede multilateral approaches. Many in the U.S. government no longer care whether others approve of or support American actions. This realization is startling to those whose habits of mind were formed during the Cold War period. Now, if the U.S. government perceives actions as in its economic or imperial interest, the administration will take these actions regardless of world opinion, including the opinion of our erstwhile allies.

Is this a sustainable policy? I think not. To some extent, the present administration is already recognizing that there is some need for international support. However, it seems more likely that the United States will pressure the United Nations to support its established policies rather than share decision making, for example, about Iraq.

The imperial project of the United States is not sustainable *ecologically*. Both its economic and its military expressions have caused irreparable harm to the environment. They have hastened the disasters that may be anticipated from global warming.

One motivation for empire is control of natural resources, especially oil. We live in the petroleum age, and we know that production will peak soon, if it has not already done so. Reduced supply and increased demand will cause the price to rise dramatically. Wars speed its depletion, so that even with military victories and greater control over oil, the prospect for the United States to maintain its present economy will grow dim. The world needs to use the remaining oil frugally and efficiently. The policies of the United States are massively wasting resources at home and abroad.

The most obviously unsustainable feature of current American policy is *financial*. The United States simply cannot continue to tax less, to spend more, and to expect the rest of the world to pay its bills. There are two ways that the rest of the world has been paying these bills. First, some nations have given a few hundred million dollars or a few billion dollars to help cover the cost of our wars. That has been very helpful, but when the United States enters a war unilaterally, without the support of the United Nations, it is less likely that many countries will grant the billions that are needed in order to pay for it and the requisite reconstruction. Others are still helping in Afghanistan, but substantial assistance with respect to the pacification and reconstruction of Iraq is not forthcoming as long as the United States insists on total control.

The second way other nations pay U.S. bills is by buying U.S. government bonds and other American assets. They thereby finance our national debt and enable us to continue deficit spending. This is not a sustainable system. First, it gives other nations great power over us, since abrupt selling of their holdings could precipitate financial chaos. Second, as the size of the debt grows, confidence in the dollar declines. There has already been a dramatic decline of the dollar in relation to other currencies. Investing in a declining currency is not attractive.

Conclusion

The imperial motive is just as important as the economic motive. That is, *economic power has been as much in the service of empire as empire has been in the service of the economic elite.* The two are inexorably tied together. If we cannot finance what we are doing, we are going to be in trouble. First, we are going to have to pay for these things ourselves, and we do not want to pay for them. Second, as we go further and further into debt, the Europeans, the Japanese, and the third-world elites are becoming less enthusiastic about buying our bonds and investing in our stock market. As the debt grows, the U.S. economy looks less stable.

Growing indebtedness is not a new phenomenon. Over recent decades it has resulted from the increasing imbalance of our international trade. We have paid for the excess of imports over exports by selling our bonds and stock and real estate to those from whom we import. We send our dollars to pay for their goods, and they invest these dollars in the United States. In short, we are exchanging our capital assets for their consumer goods. Otherwise we would have been in acute trouble long ago.

We cannot count on this arrangement continuing indefinitely. On strictly economic grounds, with our unilateralism, we have come to a point of overreach. A fiscal crisis of huge proportions could occur at any time.

We must recognize that the goals of the dominant faction in the Democratic Party are not so different from those of the Republicans. The difference is that their multilateral methods make American hegemony more acceptable and secure greater support from others. This approach makes the pursuit of empire less expensive and investment in the U.S. economy more attractive. If the Bush-Cheney administration is followed by a Democratic administration that returns to multilateral policies, the American empire may—ironically—continue much longer.

It seems likely that American overreach for power and unilateral control may bring an end to the American empire it seeks to advance and a collapse of the American economy. Because of the enormous hardships this will entail for American citizens, and especially for the poor, it is hard to view it as a hopeful prospect. What is happening in other parts of the world may provide better grounds for hope that the imperial project will end and a better order emerge. Another world *is* possible. I will address some hopeful new developments in chapter 5.

Chapter 3

Slouching toward a Fascist World Order

Richard Falk

My approach to this inquiry into the establishment of a global American empire is to ask not *whether* or *how*, but *what kind*. My underlying purpose is to identify some alternative future for world order more hopeful than a system of global dominance presided over by American hegemonic power.

The present outlook is not favorable. A former national security advisor, Zbigniew Brzezinski, believes that "[t]he only world government currently even remotely possible would be an American political dictatorship—and that would be an unstable and ultimately self-destructive enterprise."[1] For Brzezinski, the choice is "between dominating the world and leading it," the latter in the form of what he calls "a co-optive hegemony," as distinguished from the project of the Bush White House, which is labeled "assertive domination."[2] In effect, Brzezinski, along with much of the American political establishment, is interpreting the global setting as one that confers upon the United States an imperial destiny. He differs with the Bush administration only in holding that this destiny can be realized in a more acceptable and sustainable form, especially if its managerial and exploitive features are portrayed as "leadership."[3]

In opposition to this debate among factions within the imperialist camp, I am insisting that the politically defining choice is not yet so foreclosed: there remains some uncertainty as to the outcome of the struggle between imperial and cosmopolitan/democratic forces to shape the future of world order. Despite this field of struggle, the existing and emerging reality certainly seems predominantly imperial in design and effect.

This overriding impression of impending global empire partly explains the mood of political despair currently afflicting so much of humanity. Extremist and fanatical reactions to this imperial reality, epitomized by terrorist bombings in urban centers, also contribute to this pessimism about human destiny.

In addition, the refusal of major political actors, especially the United States, to take precautionary steps to ensure the ecological sustainability of the planet add to the sense of impending doom.

What Kind of Empire?

In order to raise issues relating to alternatives to empire and despair in a useful way, we first must understand the kind of empire that America seems to be establishing, whether by deliberate plan or as the byproduct of its economic, military, and diplomatic hegemony. My view is that either in its current, more militarist form, or in the more economistic/constitutional form advocated by Brzezinski and prefigured by the Clinton and Bush I presidencies, this American imperial project is an unprecedented kind of empire, which differs from all past empires in fundamental respects.

Borderless

To begin with, this empire has no boundaries. It purports to extend its authority to the entire world, although only for limited purposes. The nature of this imperial undertaking is significantly shaped by the resolve not to allow political rivals anywhere on the planet to challenge this American dominance, whether the challengers be states or nonstates. This declared intention, along with credible capability to intervene anywhere in the world to destroy political forces hostile to the imperial mandate, is a recipe for perpetual conflict.

The Hard and Soft Options

In the years between the collapse of the Berlin Wall and the 9/11 attacks, the prospect of America's choosing the soft imperial variant seemed likely to prevail. Such a demilitarized geopolitics seemed plausible in that global setting, as there appeared to be neither the disposition nor the capability on the part of any state to mount either a military or ideological challenge to America's global supremacy. Accordingly, American imperial goals could seemingly be achieved within the framework of economic globalization, although this approach was derided as naive and destined for failure during the 1990s by neoconservative think tanks—such as the American Enterprise Institute, the Heritage Foundation, and the Hoover Institution—that were beating the drums for greater reliance on force and intervention in American foreign policy.

It was difficult to contest the soft option in the relatively relaxed atmosphere of the decade following the end of the Cold War. Even George W. Bush's presidential campaign in 2000 suggested that the United States could realize its goals without going abroad in search of monsters to slay and, oddly—given our current understanding—sounded a genuinely conservative (as distinct from neoconservative) note, advocating diminished global involvement. Candidate Bush was especially critical of such liberal internationalist projects as "nation-building" and "humanitarian diplomacy," which had been hallmarks of American foreign policy during the Clinton years and which were derided by traditional conservatives as inept global philanthropy that failed to serve national interests.

The dramatic geopolitical importance of the 9/11 attacks was to expose the soft imperial option to severe disruption, thereby significantly discrediting it in elite circles. Despite this exposure, not a single established American political leader stepped forward to question the feasibility of the imperial undertaking.

In any case, the traumatizing occasion of the attacks was immediately—and suspiciously—used by the Bush White House and Pentagon to shift the geopolitical gears of American foreign policy quickly and decisively to the hard imperial option. In this regard, *Rebuilding America's Defenses*, a report of the Project for the New American Century that was released just prior to the tarnished November 2000 election (which brought George W. Bush to Washington), has correctly been viewed as of great relevance, revealing neoconservative pre-9/11 strident advocacy of the hard option and sharp criticism of the Clinton presidency because of its misguided adherence to the soft option.[4]

In an important respect, the November 2004 presidential election centered on whether, in light of the failure in Iraq, American foreign policy should pursue its imperial goals by a return to the soft option.

The Bush administration, feeling confirmed by its return to the White House, still insists on going forward with the hard option, reconfigured to some extent by the Iraq experience. "Going forward" means sticking with the strategic goals in Iraq, exerting increasing pressure on Syria on antiterrorist grounds, on Iran on the pretext of a concern about the spread of nuclear weapons, and possibly on North Korea and eventually on China as the only political actor capable of shattering American dreams of global empire. The U.S. government is likely to make a greater effort to enlist wider international support for these main initiatives by stressing a common antiterrorist agenda and pursuing its geopolitical goals in a less blatantly unilateralist manner.[5] Up to this point, the signals are mixed as to whether even the style of the Bush diplomacy during the remainder of his presidency will be more accommoda-tionist. The appointment of the blustering and reactionary bully John Bolton as U.S. representative at the United Nations suggests continued adherence during Bush's second term to an in-your-face unilateralism. The London tube and bus attacks of July 7, 2005, may lend a renewed, if temporary, credibility in the public's eye to American diplomacy based on antiterrorist solidarity.[6]

The radical innovativeness and multiple dangers of the hard imperial option as the operative foundation of American foreign policy since 9/11, as well as its far-reaching political implications, should be appreciated. The sheer scale of geopolitical ambition has given rise to unprecedented schemes for sustaining total military control of the political life of the planet. David Griffin in chapter 1 perceptively emphasizes the further militarization of space as a critical dimension of the originality of this empire, with its insistence on manifesting its lethal global reach as a mechanism for intimidation and coer-cion and as a necessary feature of its reliance on both covert and overt mili-tary action.

An Informal, Unacknowledged Empire

The emergent American empire in either of its two forms is a political nov-elty in other respects as well. This empire is distinctive to the degree that it is a self-consciously informal empire and nominally an "anti-empire." It doesn't seek to displace the formal sovereignty of other states and even claims to respect and promote the right of self-determination of all peoples—while at the same time reserving the option for itself to intervene if necessary to pro-mote "regime change." This American leadership resents any suggestion of its imperial intent or identity, continuing to invoke America's historical roots as a constitutional republic as if nothing fundamental had changed.

In one sense, to be sure, nothing *has* changed, if one views the entirety of American history as a concealed courtship with empire. Political elites in America, whether hard or soft, nearly always repudiate any insinuation of the presence of imperial ambitions, past or present (although an increasing num-ber of voices in the mainstream academic community are asking leaders to cast aside this anti-imperial political myth and to use the supposedly democ-ratic marketplace of ideas to determine what kind of empire America should become).[7]

The political approach of the Bush administration to the Iraq War is illus-trative of this American political style of diplomacy, relying on the hard impe-rial option in practice while purporting to be respectful of the sovereignty of others in rhetoric. From the outset of the Iraq War in March 2003, even when an easy victory seemed assured, the U.S. government made many statements to the effect that the sovereignty of Iraq would not be impaired by the American invasion and temporary occupation, pointing backward in time to the allegedly happy result of the Allied occupation of Germany and Japan after World War II. This tension in Iraq between deed and word was readily apparent from the first days of the occupation, perhaps best epitomized by the failure of American troops to protect Iraqi cultural treasures, including the famed national museum in Baghdad, from bands of looters, while guarding the oil fields with due diligence. All along, the United States has mischievously declared the absence of any territorial ambitions while proceeding with the construction of expensive permanent military bases in Iraq for future strategic use in the region.

There is no indication of any effort by this American leadership to revive the formal colonial era by extending its formal boundaries or authority to encompass some or all of the subordinate political communities that constitute a world of sovereign states. At the same time, there are numerous political entities that are subject to de facto American governance in different parts of the world, including several that broke away from the former Yugoslavia.

A Commitment to a Totalizing and Militarist Hegemony

The United States, claiming the right to exercise control over the entire world, has invested in the capabilities and invented legitimating rationalizations to make this a somewhat plausible project, at least among its American supporters. It proclaims for itself unconditional sovereign rights while claiming an exemption from the constraints of international law binding on normal states, so that it can violate the sovereignty of other nations. The United States has committed itself to regional navies on all the oceans of the world. It has military bases in at least sixty countries and a military presence in more than one hundred countries. It purports to have a monopoly over the militarization of space, although China is mounting a formidable challenge. The United States is by far the largest player in the international arms-sales market.

Most significantly of all, America maintains a sufficient military superiority over any state or likely combination of states, while exhibiting a strong national commitment to sustain this level of dominance as the prime expression of a bipartisan foreign policy in the new era of unipolarity initiated by the Soviet collapse. One concrete initiative that reflects this domestic consensus is the construction of a defensive missile shield, which is justified as useful for deterring, and possibly defending against, a missile attack by a third-world adversary, particularly a "rogue state," as designated by the Washington bureaucracy.[8]

As Griffin persuasively argues, it is undoubtedly the case that this space-based weapons and surveillance system is more appropriately understood as providing the United States in the near future with a panoptic global capacity to monitor behavior at any point on the planet and to be in a position to direct overwhelming force wherever and whenever the behavior of others is perceived as threatening to U.S. interests. In such a world order, American security is pursued at the cost of the permanent *insecurity* of all other states.

Such a project is unlikely to be achieved, however imposing the military edifice, because it will be challenged and discredited by a spectrum of movements of resistance—violent and nonviolent, extremist and moderate. The extremist movements will likely strike lethally at a shifting array of soft targets from a virtually limitless list of possibilities, while the moderate ones will act from within and without to undermine the credibility and sap the political will of the imperial overlords. The outcome of such an interplay is not security for the empire but insecurity for both the strong and the weak.

An element at play here is the extension of an American global reach based increasingly on overwhelming military might, along with the willingness to use force on a discretionary basis in violation of the UN Charter and international law.

This extension of the battlefield to the entire world acquired, at first, a degree of reasonableness and enjoyed the acquiescence of most governments, including even an undivided United Nations, in the immediate aftermath of 9/11. At that point, the main declared political enemy of the United States had become a nonstate global actor that, like the United States, exhibited no willingness to acknowledge the sovereign rights of other states or to respect territorial borders in the course of carrying on its struggle by extremist methods. In such a setting, most governments instinctively sided with the United States as the only state capable of defending the integrity of the Westphalian structure of world order against a nonstate, indeed an antistate, usurper that had shown a capacity and will to engage in indiscriminate violence on a massive scale. (The "Westphalian structure" is a widely used designation to identify the modern world order. This development is typically traced back to the end of the religious wars in 1648, and the name derived from the Peace of Westphalia, which signaled the emergence of the sovereign state as the primary unit of world order.)

The underlying conflict, then, between the United States and al-Qaeda is best understood as an encounter between these two global actors, each unprecedented: one representing some of the darkest violent and fanatical forces in civil society, the other representing the deterritorialization of a hegemonic state power, coupled with the assumption of postcolonial imperial prerogatives with respect to law and order.[9]

This post-9/11 statist consensus fractured badly in the period preceding the Iraq War, when it became evident to several major normally friendly foreign governments that the United States was conflating its antiterrorist struggle, for which there was widespread support, with its imperial project, for which there was very little intergovernmental support, and even less support from civil society publics around the world. The Iraq War, vividly exhibiting the priority being accorded the imperial project by the Bush administration, sent geopolitical shivers down the spine of many other world leaders and their populations, resulting in the spread of anti-Americanism far beyond the Islamic world, reaching the point where world public opinion viewed the United States as a greater menace than al-Qaeda.

But we must not ignore the genuine structural transformation that seems to be at work. The various nonstate elements of the current global setting do require interpreters to overcome their statist preconceptions so as to grasp this truly innovative reality, which is essentially nonterritorial in character.

It is helpful to recall that study of modern Westphalian international relations was based on the idea that significant international conflict took place exclusively among territorial state actors, who enjoyed sovereign rights within existing and internationally accepted boundaries. To the extent that there were departures from this image of a world order constituted by sovereign states, these were mainly based on the formal extension of state power, as occurred in the colonial system and the establishment of multinational empires, which ruled entire regions. These empires always had frontiers and boundaries, even if contested and vague in some instances.

The closest antecedent to America's global empire was probably the British Empire in the nineteenth century boasting that "the sun never sank on the Union Jack." But Britain made no claim that its power could penetrate wherever and whenever it willed, and the weaponry of the day lacked the capacity to destroy whole cities and societies with deadly accuracy at great distances. Wars were primarily military engagements between states, which took place on battlefields or at sea. Every past empire, despite the rhetoric of universalism often used, was operating within frontiers. Colonial empires of the European powers in recent centuries were multicivilizational and multicontinental, to be sure, but they were based on linkages among distinct political communities of bounded territory. Such empires were also kept in check to some extent by inter-imperial rivalries.

A Global Security State with Double Standards

In contrast, the American empire involves the emergence of what might be called a global security state—a sovereign state that insists more than any other state in the world on its own territorial sovereignty while simultaneously disregarding the sovereignty of every other state (although to varying degrees).

Imperial actors create the rules of the political game, implement them selectively, and do so without feeling uncomfortable about their double standards and the exceptions they make for themselves. If assessed by such criteria, the United States certainly qualifies as an imperial actor, and its imperial behavior can be observed in a number of critical areas. Perhaps one of the most inflammatory, with regard to events leading to 9/11, is the way in which the United Nations has been used and abused in the Palestine-Israel conflict.

There are many reasons for the deep disenchantment of the Islamic world with the West, reasons that explain why there is such wide grassroots resonance for al-Qaeda violence and extremism, even as it is repudiated at official levels throughout the Islamic world. The civic popularity of this extremism arises in large part because such anti-American transnational violence is widely regarded as the first significant display of effective resistance to the American imposition of double standards on the Islamic world. Support for this resistance is also forthcoming as a reaction to the long period of humiliating impotence of the Islamic governments, Arab governments in particular. For decades, these governments have been unable and unwilling to defend the most fundamental rights of what is viewed as the Islamic community.

Osama bin Laden initially called attention to the extremely provocative presence of American military forces deployed close to the most sacred Muslim sites on the Arabian peninsula, along with the unwillingness of the Saudi government to object to and terminate this unacceptable situation. Likely of wider significance than the issue of American military deployments for the Islamic world, which was admittedly important for bin Laden and perhaps for the initial al-Qaeda leadership, is the unresolved Palestinian struggle for self-determination, along with Israel's resistance on annexing Jerusalem.

The Israeli-Palestinian Situation

Nothing would do more to calm the passions that have existed in the world since 9/11 than a just settlement of the Palestinian claim for self-determination, especially if the United States were finally perceived as seeking an outcome that is fair to both sides rather than, as to date, pretending to be an "honest broker" while acting as an unconditional partisan and protector of Israel, the far stronger negotiating partner. If the American leadership genuinely wanted to give priority to the challenge of global terrorism, overcoming the Palestinian ordeal by realizing the national rights of the Palestinians would be at the very top of Washington's policy agenda. Such a call for a just and sustainable solution cannot be achieved by making the Palestinians swallow an unjust solution—a mini-state lacking the features of true political independence, a virtual Bantustan—and then calling this outcome "peace." Real peace requires a fair settlement enabling both peoples to live independently and with self-esteem next to one another, in a condition of formal and substantive equality or, conceivably—as has been more recently advocated in light of the extensive penetration of Palestinian territory by numerous Israeli settlements—as a single binational state organized on a federal basis with a deliberately weak central government.

I mention this particular conflict in the context of suggesting that it is characteristic of empire both to create crucial rules of the game and then to assume the prerogative of enforcing them so selectively that the impression is created of arbitrary power rather than the rule of law, much less power in the service of justice. The most elementary aspect of the rule of law is to treat equals equally, so the most direct repudiation of law (and justice) is to treat equals unequally. If power is used to treat equals unequally, especially in relation to issues of war and peace, then it exposes the role of power and domination and undermines respect for peaceful solutions of international conflicts. If justice rather than declared law is to be the moral measure of world order, then the proper test is the response to human suffering and the privations of the weak.

Weapons of Mass Destruction

Another issue in which the double standards are blatant is that of weapons of mass destruction. I am amazed that there has not been more opposition to this profoundly contradictory relationship to nuclear weaponry. I can attribute the acquiescence of the nonnuclear states only to their sense of powerlessness and hence to their geopolitical despair in recognition of the futility of their opposition.

The United States has recently waged a war allegedly to respond to threats emanating from an Iraq supposedly possessing weapons of mass destruction. It turned out, of course, that Iraq had not possessed such weapons for several years. The alleged threat provided a pretext to mobilize popular backing in the United States for a strategic war of choice that was initiated by Washington for undisclosed reasons that remain a matter of more or less informed speculation. But whatever the reasons, they were not the reasons that we as Americans were given at the time. It was, therefore, a great abuse of authority by elected officials. In a democratic society, recourse to war on the basis of deception is perhaps the greatest of all such abuses, which in a healthy democracy would produce, at minimum, a widespread call for the removal of the responsible leaders. Sending young citizens to potential and actual death and injury, while giving their elected representatives and the citizenry a fraudulent rationale for the war, should certainly be grounds for presidential and vice-presidential impeachment.

However, while this point has been made often and widely, the deeper problem is that at the very time American leaders were insisting that countries such as Iraq were not entitled to uphold their security as they saw fit, including if necessary by weapons of mass desctruction, we were continuing to violate our side of the nuclear nonproliferation treaty, in which we and other nuclear powers declared our "intention to achieve at the earliest possible date the cessation of the nuclear arms race and to undertake effective measures in the direction of nuclear disarmament."[10] Besides the fact that we have, for the thirty-eight years since the treaty entered into force, failed to undertake such measures, we were, while getting ready to attack Iraq, defiantly developing *new* nuclear weapons, including "bunker busters" and the deceptively named mini-nukes.[11]

For the United States to insist that sovereign states, especially those that are under threat, either forgo the nuclear option or face sanctions and possibly military intervention is to revise one of the most fundamental principles of modern world order based on the Westphalian logic of state equality. In the present situation, it prohibits governments from the pursuit of their national security in a manner that gives them some chance of deterring the most powerful and threatening country in the world.

To couple such a prohibition with the refusal even to consider arrangements for eliminating the American arsenal of these weapons, while at the same time increasing this arsenal, emphasizes the overtness of imperial double standards on this most crucial of all matters of global policy. The maddening arrogance of these double standards is made even worse by the fact that the United States, while being prepared to wage war against some countries because they seek nuclear weapons, evades the awkward reality that Israel has secretly developed such weapons. Israel's unchallenged arsenal of nuclear weapons communicates to other countries the harsh degree to which American pretensions of providing global leadership on the issue of nonproliferation are geopolitically motivated, self-serving, and abusive with respect to the aspirations of many of the peoples in the world.

A Bipartisan Consensus and Refusal

These world-order issues reinforce the importance of the distinction that John Cobb has drawn between unilateral and multilateral approaches to an imperial role for the United States. There is no fundamental *structural* difference between the manipulation of these double standards in the Clinton presidency and in the current presidency of George W. Bush. It is important to acknowledge the bipartisan foundation for the assertion of an American imperial identity.

So far neither imperial variant, soft or hard, has been willing to own up to its violation of the statist world order by virtue of its global imperial project or to the costs for the American people and the even greater costs for other peoples, especially in countries where the imperial regime is challenged.

Griffin quotes statements by George W. Bush and Donald Rumsfeld in which they deny that the United States seeks an empire. If we grant the sincerity of these assertions by the top American leadership, there seems present here what psychologists would identify as denial or, more obscurely, "cognitive dissonance." More plausibly, there is present a mixture of denial with political myth making, which means affirming the continuity between the present and the legitimating myth surrounding the founding of the American republic and the establishment of its constitutional framework, while at the same time pursuing a contradictory path in policy.

There remains a refusal on the part of the American elite to acknowledge the abandonment of this fundamental constitutional identity of America, being republican with a small *r*. America anchors its claims of legitimacy and exceptionalism on its early repudiation of the kind of colonial possessions that were byproducts of a Eurocentric world order. The American Revolution represented the first successful revolt against such colonial rule. Mainstream historians generally admit that America briefly embraced colonialism in the aftermath of the Spanish-American War, but they consider that experience anomalous, a temporary deviation from an abiding American anti-imperial identity.

This complex dynamic of denial and apologetics is not new. But what *is* definitely new is the extension of this dynamic to an encompassing vision of political aspiration to establish a control mechanism, validated as "global security" and "democratization," for the entire world.

The Possibility of the Imperial Project

The collapse of the Soviet Union gave this aspiration a certain geopolitical and hegemonic plausibility, in the sense of being seemingly attainable by persuasion and prestige, but above all by reliance on the militarist logic of power projection. After the Soviet collapse, no *territorial* power on the face of the earth was capable of deterring this single geographical center of power. Beyond this, the United States enjoyed the triumphalist satisfaction of its Cold War victory, which led to a rapid marketization of the entire world, most influentially and pretentiously expressed by the elaborate argument of Francis Fukuyama that the collapse of the Soviet Union heralded "the end of history," as socialism, the only remaining idea capable of challenging liberalism, had been crushed.[12]

What is most significant about the al-Qaeda mission is that it has posed a credible, and seemingly unmanageable, threat to the stable establishment of an imperial unipolar world order. This mission has also confirmed that history does indeed go on, perhaps not as before, but in a manner that involves a struggle of ideas as well as a type of warfare.

The real significance of the phasing out of strategic conflict in the Westphalian style, that is, state-to-state warfare, is that there has emerged unexpectedly a completely new modality of strategic conflict, which pits massive state power, technocratically assembled and globally deployed, against the primitive style of highly dispersed and concealed antistate political violence. This "new fact" reintroduces the issue of whether an imperial world order is a plausible political project. It was, of course, never desired or desirable for the majority of the peoples of the world, after waging a struggle against colonialism, to find themselves subordinated by another arrangement of Western dominance, especially when the security aspects of this arrangement are reinforced by patterns of economic globalization that confer disproportionate economic benefits on the rich and powerful.

The Uniqueness of Global Unipolarity

Reflecting upon the significance of unipolarity, or "the unipolar moment," also makes it evident that there is no balancing mechanism in this international order, so long as it is conceived to be a system of sovereign states. The modern state system never rested on the idea that stability and peace were achieved by mutual and consistent adherence to law and to legal norms and procedures, along with self-restraint by sovereign political actors. Stability and moderation when present at various historical intervals were regarded as exhibiting a kind of managed equilibrium, triumphs of statecraft, which adapted to changing international circumstances, especially to the rise of expansionist states, by calling for countervailing diplomatic measures. This logic meant that as soon as one state became too strong, other states would collaborate to create a defensive alliance, which would aim to achieve deterrence and containment and then, if this failed, use military action. This is what the peoples of the United States and its allies thought they were doing in relation to the Soviet Union during much of the more than four decades after World War II.[13]

The whole idea of containment and deterrence was actually in the mainstream tradition of how order and stability and to some degree peace were sustained in this world of sovereign states lacking an overall government. Its character acquired an apocalyptic dimension due to the advent of nuclear weaponry, which essentially undermined war as a rational option in the spectrum of diplomatic responses even in the event that the balance failed, but since this circumstance affected both sides, it increased the stability of the balance, but with a great heightening of risk in the event of failure. This balance-of-power mechanism had operated historically ever since states were unified and exercised an effective monopoly on taxing power and legitimate violence.[14]

The present situation, which is very much affected by the absence of deterrence, raises in acute form, and on an unprecedented (planetary) scale, the issue of power and geopolitical hubris to which Griffin refers in quoting the influential maxim of Lord Acton on the corrupting impact of power.[15]

Has there ever existed any worldly center of power that can be trusted, internally or externally, if it has no checks and balances operating to contain its use of that power? As shown by *The National Security Strategy of the United States* issued in 2002 (known as *NSS 2002*) and the major speeches of President Bush, especially the West Point speech of that same year, the primary security commitment of this administration is to invest sufficiently in military superiority so that no country or nonstate actor anywhere on the face of the earth can succeed as a challenger.[16]

This commitment to military dominance over all others is not limited to the so-called axis-of-evil countries or to countries that harbor terrorists for which such global reach would not be needed. To the extent that traditional military capabilities control the modalities of political relationships, it is a long-term posture that makes sense only if it is aimed at traditional states and other political formations that might otherwise be tempted to challenge American primacy. Perhaps there is also a conceptual lag at work here, resulting in an unwarranted confidence that traditional military dominance can also defeat nonstate adversaries. In any case, the scale and nature of the huge military budget confirm an imperial ambition looking toward an enduring and nationally advantageous solution to the problem of security, while also providing self-serving global governance administered from Washington. Whether the U.S. government has adopted a tolerable and effective means to attain these goals is open to debate and subject to growing doubts, but the existence of this imperial intention is beyond debate.

Fascist and Democratic Responses to Crisis

As global warming and ecological decline become more severe, there would be, initially at least, a drift towards authoritarian, even fascist, solutions that preserve the privileged hierarchy of access to world resources.[17] Such a circumstance of heightened awareness would also prompt democratizing forces, as Griffin has elsewhere suggested,[18] to be more sensitive to the political and ecological dangers of acquiescence and, therefore, to mount greater resistance.

All the evidence that we now possess suggests that in elite circles, environmental and resource scarcities will accentuate the hierarchical character of world order rather than generate moves toward greater equality and more reliance on cooperation. The first President Bush famously declared on the eve of the Earth Summit, held in Rio de Janeiro under UN auspices in 1992, that whatever the environmental situation, "the American way of life was not negotiable." This was itself a rather imperial expression of an incredible position—that although human survival might be endangered, the bloated American standard of living (and waste) would not be reduced. Such moral and political decadence with respect to human destiny has rarely been so openly embraced.

It may also be useful to consider whether this deepening global crisis of sustainability accounts for part of this American impulse to establish a global empire under its authority. For it is only by means of imperial authority that the rising challenge of global governance can be met in an age of ecological fragility and resource scarcity, especially with respect to fossil fuels, without jeopardizing the privileged American lifestyle based on illusions of unending material abundance.[19] This authoritarian scenario will be momentarily disguised as a necessary security adjustment to the threats of global terrorism. Whatever the rationale, it is neither a pleasant nor a practical solution to sustainability or security for anyone in the world, including ourselves.[20] Global authoritarianism under American control does offer a coherent solution that is likely to be tested by experience and challenged by resistance unless it manages to self-destruct—or is superseded by a democratic alternative.

In any event, the global empire scenario will, due to the complexity of globalizing trends and deteriorating conditions arising from political fragmentation, give rise to a parallel movement led by forces of global civil society to establish an institutionalized form of global governance that is more equitable than has ever previously existed. Whether the needed global political imaginary can be fashioned within sufficient time, then achieve sufficient leverage to prevent ecological collapse, is an open question.

The further originality of a hierarchical global empire is that, as earlier discussed, its full flowering is being prefigured through the medium of "a war" between actors that has no boundaries, proceeds in a framework without agreed limits, and has no clear statement of an acceptable outcome.

Subsequent historians and commentators on the international scene may regard the present pattern of conflict as a traumatic preparation for global political unification. This kind of unification will seem, when it occurs, to be functionally connected with the need for some kind of centralized governance, which the traditional system of sovereign states proved incapable of providing.[21] These underlying trends toward global governance have a historical relevance that has been submerged beneath the renewed preoccupation with global security since 9/11 and by heightened opposition to the American response.[22]

Michael Ignatieff has argued the liberal case for using American imperial power (which he accepts as a potentially benevolent reality) to implement human rights, to promote democracy, and to practice a humanitarian diplomacy. It is clarifying to take note of the title of Ignatieff's most influential statement of this theme: "The Burden of Empire."[23] Now that an American empire exists, he argues, the only useful debate concerns *how* this imperial power is to be exercised. Ignatieff portrays himself as one who is trying his best to reconcile imperial policies and structures with liberal values. The result, however, is a co-opted and corrupted discourse that focuses on the supposed uncertainty as to whether this empire will act in a totally reactionary way, by which he means the hard, unilateralist, option of Bush and the neoconservatives, or on behalf of more positive purposes, by which he means the soft, more multilateralist, option of the Clinton Democrats. It is irresponsible, at best, for Ignatieff to write as if the current American leadership, even if it were pursuing the soft option, might pursue a benevolent course.

It is misleading to claim that the structure of international life is for better or worse now best characterized as a pattern of domination, which can be maintained only by this global state, and that only this global state is capable of providing an acceptable level of world order. The widespread dissemination and acceptance of this belief in mainstream America, including the media, is one of the principal reasons that the global American empire, as idea and project, is likely to prove quite resilient, even though its rhetorical existence will continue to be vigorously denied by most political leaders. Had the Bush-Cheney administration been defeated in the 2004 elections, this quest for global empire would not have been renounced.

This defeat would also not have altogether removed the menace of what I call the prospect of global *fascism*. I use this term partly as a deliberate provocation, but partly because it suggests the depth of the danger we face if the present imperial consensus is not repudiated *in America*. American foreign

policy in a Kerry presidency would have most likely devoted its primary energies to the continued construction of a post-Westphalian empire under the ultimate control of Washington and would, therefore, have persisted with
unabated fury to sustain the occupation of Iraq.

True, such a leadership would certainly have attempted to downshift its
geopolitical rhetoric and some of its practice, signaling a renewed American
intention to seek goals of global governance multilaterally and exhibiting a
more convincing commitment to the global public interest in security and sustainability. This soft option would almost certainly not have significantly
diminished the intensity of anti-imperial resistance in the Arab world, because
it has arisen in response to a series of legitimate grievances that, as Kerry
emphatically confirmed during and after the presidential campaign, he would
have treated in the same manner as Bush.[24]

The Specter of Fascism

I turn now to why I consider it important to express concern about the present
political drift by relying on the admittedly inflammatory language of fascism.

It would be irresponsible to overlook the fascist implications of the worldview of George W. Bush, Dick Cheney, and many other leading members of
their administration, but it would also be unjustified to suppose that a mainstream alternative leadership from either political party would relieve us altogether of this prospect. The specter of fascism arose in light of several very
troubling elements that, having assumed significance immediately after 9/11,
have persisted despite exposure and criticism.

The mobilization for war by the strongest country in the world, around a
patriotic creed based on a mixture of fear and anger resulting from the 9/11
attacks, convinced a majority of Americans that it was necessary for national
security to project American power around the world in times and places of
the government's choosing, while at the same time tightening the screws of
governmental control domestically in the name of "homeland security."

Such a globalizing posture encountered stiff resistance and opposition in
global civil society from the outset of the Bush presidency, and it intensified
as America responded with war against sovereign states rather than law
enforcement directed at the nonstate network allegedly responsible for the
9/11 attacks. This civic opposition, which became more active and visible in
the period before the Iraq War, was increased by the failure of the UN Security Council to endorse American invasion plans, despite immense geopolitical pressures. The defection of such Cold War allies as France and Germany

was particularly notable. The antiwar demonstrations of February 15, 2003, a month before the Iraq War, held in some eighty countries and involving as many as 11 million demonstrators, were dismissed by Bush as "focus groups." In fact, such a global display of civic opposition and transnational solidarity in advance of a particular war had never occurred before.

In spite of this unprecedented show of opposition, Bush's decision to go ahead with his war policy had a basis in an imperialist impulse rooted in American history. As argued earlier, this impulse has recently been reinforced by a national consensus on security requirements in the twenty-first century. This consensus is continually comforted by an ultranationalist and patrioteering affirmation of the United States as the best country in the world. Such nationalist pretensions make little effort to hide the incredible conceit that, to the extent that interventionary diplomacy by the United States succeeds, it will benefit people everywhere.

In other words, this militarization of America's missionary impulse has involved no admission of its exploitative character, a fact not solely a consequence of the ascendancy of the neoconservatives. They do, however, express the strategic rationale in its crudest and most unconditional form, ringing alarm bells at home and abroad. But it is widely claimed, especially by resurgent religious evangelists, that the establishment of a benign imperial world order would represent the practice of a responsible international morality, because the United States would be bringing a better life and superior values to the rest of the world.

This moral claim is accompanied by the view, widely shared among Americans, that the United States could maintain its military dominance for the indefinite future and that to do so would be a worthy investment in world order and national security. In this way, military dominance can be supported without acknowledging geopolitical preeminence as a strategic goal.

However, the Project for the New American Century's 2000 document, *Rebuilding America's Defenses*, was crystal clear about the importance of achieving such geopolitical preeminence. The same individuals have generally avoided such an explicit avowal of their strategic intentions since they have been in power, but their behavior has removed any hope that, after they were in power, their outlook might become more moderate. Even the difficulties of the Iraq occupation seem not to have shaken their faith in, or altered their vision of, geopolitical preeminence, although it may have led to some reconsideration of tactics and almost certainly induced a recalculation of costs.

This hard form of imperialism, unlike the soft option, makes no attempt to be sensitive to lingering feelings of sovereignty and national identity in other countries. *NSS 2002*, referred to earlier, advised China to forgo the development of military capabilities beyond what is reasonable for internal security, saying that Beijing should instead concentrate its capital investments on expanding trade and development. China was paternalistically instructed that it would be foolish and futile to waste its resources by trying to challenge American military superiority even within its own regional surroundings. China was advised that it could best advance its own interests by relying for its security on this single center of military dominance administered in Washington. It is an extraordinary message, which must have been read by Chinese leaders with amazement and consternation.

This hard option is geopolitically ambitious. It corresponds at the global level to Max Weber's notion of the state as having a monopoly of legitimate violence. America now claims that it possesses an effective monopoly over legitimate force in the world as a whole and will continue to do so into the indefinite future. This attitude also encouraged the United States to ignore the United Nations, ignore international law, and ignore allies. This attitude implies a claim to be a world government—an implicit claim that must be extremely threatening to other governments and offensive to people outside of the United States.

America's concentration of military capabilities was reinforced by the assertion, particularly by President Bush, that the adversaries of America—which means those who oppose its way of running the world—were evil or at least unconscious accomplices of evil. The axis-of-evil rhetoric was deliberately deployed by the Bush leadership on several occasions, starting in 2002, to portray the war unleashed after 9/11 as one between the forces of good and evil—a portrayal aimed at justifying a military punishment for any country that did not align itself with the United States. A further argument in support of such a rigid position was that there was no way to negotiate with this enemy, since it was not a state and had no address. American leaders also insisted that this terrorist network does not accept international humanitarian law or any limitations on the means or goals of struggle, so that its extermination is the only solution. There is no obligation to respect sovereignty, because the very survival of "civilization" is at stake.

In this struggle between these two nonterritorial political actors, each side apparently shares the belief that the only way to end the conflict is to destroy the other side. So understood, each side conceives of itself as the vehicle of the good and of its adversary as evil. This logic validates any level of violence that is deemed effective. Because the stakes are so high, neither side recognizes an obligation to respect civilian innocence, arguing that there is no true innocence for those somehow associated with the evil adversary.

The imperial side talks about terrorism, but it refuses to acknowledge the reality of *state* terrorism, although states as well as these nonstate groups fail to respect civilian innocence. The U.S. government, pretending that it never targets civilians, labels all civilian casualties of its firepower, however implausibly, as "collateral damage." The U.S. disregard of the core imperative of international humanitarian law to protect the civilian population during a military occupation is further shown by the Pentagon's refusal to collect data on Iraqi civilian casualties. The world has literally seen that even torture becomes routine and mandated as antiterrorism, justified by government officials in Washington, who play language games that fool almost no one outside America. By an objective understanding of terrorism, in sum, both sides are engaged in terrorist activities on a grand scale, with an unrestrained willingness to remove obstacles to their goals and to destroy any resistance.

For all these reasons, I consider it reasonable to think of something one might call "global fascism" as the mentality of those seeking to regulate the world, from either above or below, according to their extremist beliefs. It is easy to appreciate the extremism and the fascist implications of the jihadists, but difficult to admit our own.

Our own fascism is not, of course, the fascism that ravaged Europe in the 1930s, which was operative only on the level of the state. This new political phenomenon is a totalism on the level of a global state or empire—a totalism that arises, in part, to overcome an alleged crisis of democratic governance.[25]

This concern is given extra resonance by the fact that we have had attorneys general during the Bush presidency who have seemed fully prepared to abridge the traditional liberties of American citizens whether or not the intrusion made sense from the perspective of meeting genuine security challenges. As many people have pointed out, moreover, the USA PATRIOT Act was on the shelves of the Justice Department long before 9/11, ready to be submitted to Congress as soon as the political opportunity arose, rather than reflecting a carefully calibrated and genuine response to the attacks of 9/11.

This heightened security concern also situates a religious, racial enemy by a selective and highly prejudicial emphasis on threats posed by Muslim males. This de facto process of racial profiling as a way of giving ultranationalism and patriotism a racist and religious dimension may not be obvious to most Americans, but it is certainly perceived in the rest of the world as part of the way in which the United States has responded to the attacks of 9/11. There exists a very serious risk that if this policy succeeds, a kind of global fascism would be established, probably not as a matter of conscious design but more likely as a side effect of suppressing, domestically and internationally, the inevitable militant resistance to the hard option of imperial geopolitics.

This resistance has already exhibited a sustained fury in reaction to the American-led occupation of Iraq. The dogmatically self-serving view that America is the benevolent vehicle of history, of virtue, and of civilization, so that its enemies are the embodiment of evil, leads American ideologues automatically to portray anti-imperial resistance as a species of "terrorism." This self-vindicating discourse has been evident in the American response to Iraqi resistance, prompting an escalation of oppressive violence in the vain effort to defeat the insurgency. We can expect an escalating cycle of violence between those who continue to push toward this sort of imperial world order and those who are most fanatical in resisting and opposing its establishment.

The Reduction of the Danger

Although this danger of fascism persists, it seems somewhat reduced, at least temporarily, for several reasons.

The Iraq War

The U.S. government expected quick and total victory in the Iraq War. Failure to achieve this has been an obvious obstacle to the wider American plan for the Middle East. The fact that this war was prematurely declared over ("mission accomplished") shows that the Bush administration misunderstood the difference between prevailing on the battlefield and achieving a political victory, which alone could be accurately described as winning the war.

The American people were misled about Iraq by their elected leaders. These leaders, in turn, seemed misled by the results of the Kosovo War and the first Gulf War.

In 1991, the first President Bush appeared to understand that he could claim to have defeated the "Vietnam syndrome"—the reluctance to use American military power as an instrument of foreign policy—only if he stopped the war at the Iraqi border, curtailing in the process any strategic goals associated with regime change in Baghdad. At the time, he was persuasively criticized for describing Saddam Hussein as a demonic figure, like Hitler, while not removing him from power. One can hardly imagine ending World War II with Germany devastated but Hitler and the Nazi party still governing Germany, then describing such a result as a victory. George H. W. Bush understood the high costs of political restructuring as a goal of war, both from Vietnam and from the experience of the Reagan presidency in Lebanon in the early 1980s. Remembering that the killing of 242 Marines in Lebanon resulted in a rapid U.S. withdrawal from the country, the elder Bush was content to achieve the removal of Iraq from Kuwait and the weakening of Iraq by a punishing bombing campaign.

The Bush II leadership obviously thought that the Iraq War was more like Kosovo than Vietnam.

In Kosovo in 1999, a genuinely beleaguered population welcomed an external military presence to protect itself from ethnic cleansing at the hands of Serbia. Despite the brutality of the Saddam Hussein regime, the Iraqi people, especially the Sunnis, who had been running the country, were not receptive to foreign intervention, and certainly not to prolonged foreign occupation. The idea that a non-Muslim country, especially the United States, could pose as a liberator and occupy Iraq indefinitely was quite absurdly arrogant. It also was foolish to think that military superiority on the battlefield could overcome resistance to a hostile occupation by a foreign army. This failure in Iraq has definitely, at least for the foreseeable future, undermined the ambitions of the Rumsfeld-Wolfowitz view of restructuring the whole Middle East by mounting diplomatic pressure backed by threats of further military interventions in the region, if needed. Given the difficulties in Iraq, even a reelected Bush has had difficulty actively pursuing the hard option, although there is no sign of its abandonment.

We are witnessing an increasing criticism of the Iraq policy within America as it becomes more evident that the Iraqi resistance is not likely to be crushed or wither away and that the attempt to prevail in Iraq is imposing heavy burdens on the United States and deeply compromising its stature as global leader. The cost in money and blood already expended in Iraq is just too high for a growing sector of the public, and the belief is spreading that Bush visionaries are guilty of overextension. This belief is producing a political backlash that is beginning to worry even some Republican loyalists. This weakness of the American position was further underscored by the willingness of the Bush administration to approach the United Nations on bended knee to obtain help after earlier giving the organization an ultimatum to support the American policy on Iraq or find itself irrelevant. In returning to the United Nations in 2004 to tell the assembled governments that the UN is relevant, Bush did not, of course, repudiate the Iraq War or even admit miscalculating its difficulty. As a result, the American plea for burden sharing in the Iraqi reconstruction went unheeded.

The Economic Dimension

John Cobb lucidly analyzes the economic aspects of this imperial venture. It is somewhat ironic that an American secretary of the treasury would be sent to China, as was the case in 2004, to ask the Chinese to revalue their currency upwardly so that their exports would become more expensive for the United States.

This is an astounding step backward for a country that supposedly champions free trade and deference to market forces. What we are really saying to China is that we can no longer afford to buy (and benefit from) their cheaper goods because we are unable to compete, leaving our products unsold or sold at a loss. Because of this, we ask our Chinese competitors to raise artificially the prices of their exports so we can diminish our trade deficit and not be faced with a weakening dollar that could trigger an American economic collapse. This show of weakness is dangerously and mindlessly inconsistent with the pretension of being an imperial power of global scope.

The Loss of Credibility and Legitimacy

For a large number of people in the United States and practically everyone everywhere else, American global leadership no longer has either legitimacy or credibility. This problem emerged in the latter stages of the Vietnam War, but it now exists in a far more serious form. With regard to credibility, there is clearly a huge gap between the limits of American power and what the government says. When a government initiates a war expecting an easy victory and then proves unable to reach a favorable outcome after years of effort, it is likely that a backlash will occur and that many people will turn against a foreign policy that they previously supported. With regard to legitimacy, it has become increasingly known by the American public that neoconservative advocates of the hard option played complicated and sophisticated games with our minds, and as a result lots of people are dying. All of these factors make the Bush-Cheney administration more vulnerable than previously and make less likely the overt kind of political extremism that seemed to be almost certain if the Iraq war had been as easy as we were told it would be. Success in Iraq, according to the Bush-Cheney-Rumsfeld game plan, would have definitely led to further interventionary efforts of political restructuring via wars of choice.[26]

Bush also lost political leverage by undertaking a major push at the start of his second term to reform Social Security in a manner that divided his own party and alienated part of his political base, giving his administration less room to maneuver on foreign policy. Of course, a renewed sense of terrorist menace, due to additional terrorist attacks—such as those in London on July 7, 2005—could alter the climate in ways that make the hard option once more politically viable. At this point, however, Bush's declining support makes further aggressive moves overseas unlikely unless a new climate of urgency arises as a result of further attacks on U.S. territory.

Conclusion

Even if we succeed in repudiating the neoconservative political leadership, the United States will for a long time remain the dominant political, economic, and military actor in the world and will seek to assert global control by relying on some combination of diplomacy and coercion. There is no indication what-soever that a "moderate" alternative to the Bush-Cheney administration will abandon the weaponization of space, or give up the effort to control the global economy by deference to Wall Street and Davos,[27] or address legitimate griev-ances pertaining to American policy (starting with the Israel/Palestinian conflict and world poverty and disease), or take steps toward nuclear disarmament, or work toward the creation of a stronger and more independent United Nations, or respond to intensifying ecological challenges.

All of these moves, which would improve America's standing in the world, would be quite feasible, but there is, as of yet, no political disposition to give up the quest for global governance based on American imperial capability. The only debate in elite American circles concerns whether the pursuit of empire should rely primarily on the unilateral and militaristic or emphasize multilateral and economistic means to the extent possible.

It remains important to replace the present highly ideological, militarist, utilateralist approach to global empire as soon as possible. It would, however, be foolishly complacent to suppose that doing so would do anything more than provide a breathing spell. We would still face the challenges from peo-ple in other countries based on legitimate grievances rooted in American hegemony, and the unwillingness to associate our leadership with a commit-ment to a just world order. The persistence of global poverty, along with the enormous disparity between rich and poor, is widely—and, to a considerable extent, rightly, as John Cobb shows—perceived in the third world as a byprod-uct of American leadership. There seems to be no will in mainstream Amer-ica to acknowledge, much less address, such problems in the manner that might inspire American leaders to create the political preconditions for global democracy.

In the next chapter, I discuss a crucial question that is overlooked in most discussions of the future: Is it possible for American citizens and the peoples of the world to create an alternative to global empire unless drastic steps are taken to end the role of the war system as the basis for global security? Is war as a social institution a decisive obstacle on the path that might lead to a peace-ful and equitable future world order?

PART II

Alternatives to
the American Empire

Chapter 4

Renouncing Wars of Choice:
Toward a Geopolitics of Nonviolence

Richard Falk

We live in a world in which preparation for war and war itself are still considered normal features of world politics. This normalcy was challenged in different ways by the major wars of the twentieth century, but without major effect. Since 9/11, this normalcy has again been challenged by a spectacular and unprecedented display of the capability and resolve of nonstate actors to inflict severe harm on sovereign states and their civilian societies, even on the militarily strongest state in human history. Although war has seemed irrational since the creation of nuclear weapons if not earlier—with their catastrophic, even apocalyptic, properties—ideas about the normalcy of war have persisted.

Such weaponry should never have been used and, once used, should have been outlawed. Instead, with the war system remaining resilient, nuclear weaponry evolved and was stockpiled, and the superpower rivals in the Cold War seemed fully prepared, if attacked or sufficiently provoked, to launch a massive suicidal war.

With good reason we condemn suicide bombers who kill dozens in Sri Lanka, Palestine, Iraq, and Britain, yet we rarely contemplate our own "civilized" readiness to sacrifice millions of our own citizens and murder millions of innocent persons in foreign countries. We mask the reality of such suicidal and terrorizing missions with anesthetizing language, thereby remaining detached from our willingness to embrace death on a huge scale for the sake of often remote and abstract geopolitical goals, disguised as "defense" or "security."[1] The stark fact is that for more than half a century, both suicidal doctrines and megaterrorism have been integral to U.S. strategic doctrines of national security. Such a posture has produced only periodic dissent at the margins of civil society. For the mainstream, including the media, this national readiness to commit mass suicide and engage in terrorism on a grand scale has been treated as *morally*, *politically*, and *legally* unproblematic.

Even the briefest reflection, however, reveals our self-righteous repudiation of comparable tactics by nonstate actors, such as jihadists, as "barbaric" to be at best propagandistic. Violence against civilians has not, of course, been presented in the West as acceptable if done by the "just" side. But the one-sided repudiation of enemy violence as "terror" deflects our understanding of the absolutist methods of engaging in political conflict, thereby obstructing the adoption of consistent attitudes toward political violence and its abatement.

At the start of the twenty-first century, the war reflex seems to be hardwired into the nervous system of many governments of sovereign states and their populations. In the United States, there were no official voices calling out for caution and reflection, let alone the adoption of practical alternatives to war, in the aftermath of 9/11.

Albert Einstein famously said that the atomic bomb "changed everything except our way of thinking." The transformative collective violence unleashed by the atomic bomb was manifested in a different modality by 9/11, which dramatized, at least apparently, the unmanageable vulnerability of the powerful to the weaponry and tactics of the weak, the fanatical, and the resentful. This vulnerability was then confirmed—again, at least apparently—by subsequent attacks in Bali, Casablanca, Madrid, and London. Such a new reality should call forth new ways of thinking, feeling, and acting as a matter of urgency, without which we are likely to have a very dark future. But Einstein's illuminating comment can, in updated form, be repeated today.

As with the atomic bomb, megaterrorism is above all a challenge to the imagination, as the old methods of warrior strength and superior means of destruction are virtually irrelevant. They may actually make matters worse, by increasing the risks and consequences of military retaliation without diminishing the threat. In this regard, it is certainly plausible to believe that the American invasion of Iraq has heightened, not diminished, the likelihood of even more deadly jihadist attacks on urban centers in the West. This point cannot be dismissed as a retroactive assessment. It was predictable in advance.

It is worth asking where we might be as a nation and a species if we had accepted the fact that war has become lethally dysfunctional—that is, if, after almost six decades since the dropping of atomic bombs, we had finally changed our way of thinking with respect to national security.

Renouncing Wars of Choice

I will propose in this chapter that war is now dysfunctional, but will do so modestly, limiting the assertion of systemic dysfunction to "wars of choice"—that is, wars that cannot be convincingly justified by either defensive or humanitarian necessity and are hence undertaken for strategic reasons in violation of international law and the Charter of the United Nations. Renouncing wars of choice would not mean fully repudiating the war/security nexus. But it would involve a dramatic upgrading of trust in peaceful methods of dispute settlement and a long-overdue downgrading of war as a rational and beneficial use of power. It would represent a significant step toward acknowledging what any visitor from another solar system would immediately realize: that war, once the glory of tribes and nations, has become, due to the march of technology, an elixir of mass death and little more—at least from the perspective of producing security.[2]

But why not address the fundamental dysfunction of the war system as such, rather than merely one manifestation of it? My response, admittedly not entirely satisfactory, is that a challenge to this system as a whole would at this time be futile, given the persistent strength of war consciousness. Responsible political thought dedicated to change should be directed toward those aspects of reality that seem most susceptible to positive adjustment without a utopian change of heart.

A rejection of "wars of choice" seems like a timely project in the current world setting for several interlocking reasons: (1) Wars of choice cannot be reconciled with international law, including the core commitment of the UN Charter, prohibiting a state's recourse to force except in self-defense, narrowly defined.[3] (2) Wars of defensive or humanitarian necessity, by contrast, are difficult to eliminate without the parallel development of a system of global governance with adequate peacekeeping capabilities. (3) The strategic failure of the Iraq War invites skepticism about the rationality of wars of choice because the attempt to achieve foreign policy goals by means of this war has resulted in such disproportionate human and material costs, including an increase of the transnational terrorist threat.[4] (4) There is a mismatch between war logic, based on conflict between sovereign states, and antiterrorist logic, involving the interplay between concealed social forces and a global state that does not respect the sovereignty of other states.

Combining prudential, principled, and pragmatic considerations under current world conditions builds a strong case for the repudiation of wars of choice as a geopolitical option for leaders of powerful states. Their voluntary acceptance of such a constraint would contribute to a renewed search for security under conditions of increasing globalization.

The Realist Obstacle to Adjustment

The major obstacle to this proposal is the fact that "realist" thinking, deeply inscribed in the collective political consciousness of leaders and citizens, sets the operative outer boundaries for "responsible" political thought. Realist thinking has assumed a variety of forms during the period of Westphalian world order, generally understood to have existed from 1648 (the end of the Thirty Years War) until 1989 (the fall of the Berlin Wall). I will distinguish four inter-twined and overlapping kinds of realist thinking about world politics that have in common a focus on the decisive influence of the distribution and use of *power*, contending that the threat of war maintains order within the "anarchy" of international relations. Realist thinking also shares the conviction that anti-war thinking is irrelevant or worse, actually contributing to the onset of war.

Balance-of-Power Realism

The first type of realism, very prominent in the past two centuries, rested on the belief that the best way to address war/peace issues was to seek and main-tain a balance of power among the leading states. This mechanism of a balance or equilibrium, said to facilitate moderation by diminishing the incentives of war, was always susceptible to disruption by the emergence of revolutionary states, changing perceptions of relative power, and technological and doctri-nal innovations. The possibility of such developments was enough to encour-age ambitious leaders to try to improve their relative position by threatening or actually waging war. In this balancing schema, only states were treated as important political actors. They were deemed dedicated solely to maximizing their own vital interests, hence unwilling to subordinate their foreign policies to the mandates of law or morality. They were inhibited in resorting to war, if at all, only by their perceptions of countervailing power. This kind of realism posited an anarchical world, meaning one that lacked world government or even a transnational bonding of civil society forces.[5]

This Hobbesian framing of international relations encouraged paradoxical approaches to peace and order. The master realist statesman of recent times, Henry Kissinger, never tired of invoking the seemingly cynical Roman maxim "If you seek peace, prepare for war." This way of thinking operated as accepted wisdom throughout the multipolar world of the early twentieth cen-tury, in which there were several centers of power, and then in the Cold War, which involved a bipolar structure seeking balance—appropriately labeled a "balance of terror"—through a combination of deterrence (threats) and con-tainment (defensive capabilities and credibility).

Structural Realism

A second body of realist thought emphasizes the structure of international society at a given time. This structural realism calls attention to the number of poles of power with the capacity to project power beyond the limits of their own territory. This number has varied in modern times, but structural realists have been mostly concerned with the multipolar relations among a few great powers and, in the period between 1945 and 1989, with the bipolar interaction of the two superpowers.

Imperial Realism

Now that there is a unipolar world, with only one major center of power, these earlier forms of realist thinking seem irrelevant. As might be expected, the conceptualizing has shifted from the traditional realist discourse to various accounts of an imperial world order and its consequences for security and war/peace concerns.[6] Structural and balance-of-power realism have now been displaced by what might be called "imperial realism."

This mode of thinking focuses on the requirements of prudent and effective "governance" (a term best understood here as an upgrading of "management"). This imperial view of governance purports to be committed to establishing a peaceful world—albeit one preceded by a vaguely contoured multiphase war that grandiosely promises to end political evil by eliminating terrorism and intervening to produce regime change wherever existing governments are seen to threaten American strategic plans for global security.[7] Some imperial realists opposed the Iraq War by invoking the prudential virtues of restraint and the calculation of costs versus gains, but this prudential thinking is rejected by the visionary imperial realists in the Bush entourage.

President Bush, in his covering message attached to *NSS 2002*, made the following foolishly optimistic assertion:

> Today the international community has the best chance since the rise of the nation-state in the 17th century to build a world in which great powers compete in peace instead of continually preparing for war. Today the world's great powers find themselves on the same side. We are also increasingly united by common values. The U.S. will use this moment of opportunity to extend the benefits of freedom across the globe. We will actively work to bring the hope of democracy, the development of free markets and free trade to every corner of the world.[8]

This statement assumes that reasonable projections about the future can be made while focusing solely on the relations between leading states. This ignores the rise of nonstate actors and of transnational political movements, which are the main centers of opposition to the hierarchical and exploitative system of world order that operates under the control of the United States.

Bush's strained use of the terminology of peace, in any case, reflects the version of realism that, conceiving of power in a largely militarist sense, regards the exercise of such power as the foundation of peace. *NSS 2002* later specifies, in fact, that American military dominance is what makes possible this peaceful world—this *Pax Americana*.

The label "imperial realism" seems, therefore, to fit. The specific form of this vision offered by the United States claims that a side benefit of the concentration of power in America will be the dissemination of the values and way of life embodied in America's domestic political and economic order. With a notable disregard of historical realities and legacies (slavery, ethnocide, interventionism), President Bush blandly assumes that the entire world, if given the chance, will be quite content to live under American dominion if it can at the same time enjoy an American way of life, most positively understood as constrained sovereignty offset by unrestrained consumerism.

Before becoming president, Bush did not travel abroad very much. He continues to exhibit little interest in or knowledge about the diversities that exist on all levels of human existence. Immediately after 9/11, he posed the haunting question with respect to America's enemies, "Why do they hate us?" But instead of providing an illuminating answer, he answered his question in a most self-serving way, insisting that they hate us because they envy what we have, especially our freedom. According to this explanation, anti-Americanism is not based on any legitimate grievances. This avoidance of self-scrutiny, while strategically convenient, is one demonstration of the inability of imperial realism under American leadership to construct a stable world order.

Marxist Realism

A fourth variant of realism is rooted in the Marxist tradition, as modified by Leninism and Maoism. Although Marxist realism generates only mild interest at present, it clarifies some aspects of economic globalization in ways that touch on the persistence of war.

Like the Bush administration view just considered, Marxist realism believes that a just and peaceful world will come about only after forces of evil have been violently eliminated. For Marxists of most persuasions, political violence is the only way to overcome economic structures of privilege and exploitation, which are based on the willingness of the capitalist class to repress and mislead the masses. International wars arise continually as rival centers of capital forever press against one another in their search for larger market shares. Each entrepreneur must expand continuously to avoid collapse in the face of this competition. The state, which functions as a service agency for capitalist imperatives, is sometimes led into conflicts that escalate into vicious wars, albeit with their economistic underpinnings unacknowledged.

The realist essence of this outlook was expressed in Mao's notorious statement, "Power comes out of the barrel of a gun." Without a willingness to rely on transforming violence, this outlook says, there will be neither peace nor justice in the world, but only an oppressive status quo. This Marxist/Leninist/ Maoist worldview, which focuses on revolutionary struggles within the state, connects international war primarily with outward manifestations of a capitalist political economy. Completely cynical with respect to law and morality, it dismisses all normative claims—except its own, of course—as hypocritical disguises for the geopolitical pursuit of class interests. History is interpreted as a series of inevitable collisions between contradictory social forces.

The Realist Consensus

These four versions of realism continue to influence the way most people think about war, security, and change. The realist consensus is further reinforced by discrediting idealism as an alternative view of how to manage world politics. This discrediting reflects several twentieth-century developments.

The idealist position supposed that progress in social and political relations was more or less assured by the continuous process of scientific discovery and technological innovation. This view, reflecting the materialist understanding of human destiny fostered by the European Enlightenment, assumed that life circumstances would get gradually better as the rigors of scarcity were mitigated by an economics of abundance, which would spread wealth downward and outward to the poor. According to this teleology, human experience proceeds in an ascending spiral of achievement. An evolutionary process is at work that leads to a longer and more satisfying life for more and more people. This teleology encouraged visions of a brighter future as an effortless side effect of the passage of time, with neither class struggle nor revolution needed.

Influential historical assessments of human fallibility substantially discredited this vision. According to these assessments, the capacities for destruction have evolved far more rapidly than the attitudes and values needed for their control and mutual benefit. With the advent of weapons of mass destruction and the awareness of global pollution, the societal impacts of science and technology were negatively reevaluated. In an abrupt reversal, the relentless march of science now gave rise to a dark pessimism about human destiny.

The idealistic vision of progress also seemed oblivious to the relevance of material scarcities, which have led to widening disparities of wealth and poverty, a dynamic that was itself related to the recurrence of war.

The international high-water mark of international idealism was undoubtedly the movement led by U.S. President Woodrow Wilson after World War I to overcome the war system by establishing a collective security system embedded in the League of Nations. Wilsonian idealism, which rejected realism by resting peace on international legal norms and procedures leading to a disarmed world, radically underestimated the resilience of war as a social institution embedded in the state system. It failed, in other words, to appreciate the extent to which nationalism, sovereignty, and war making are inextricably connected in the dominant political culture of many countries, including Europe, where decades of regional integration have weakened such connections.

Wilson's visionary insistence on the possibility and necessity of an alternative to war had one success: It reshaped in an enduring manner the political imagination as to world order. The imagining of a world without war has persisted and assumed even more ambitious forms in recent decades.

Realists, however, accused Wilsonian ideas of having a detrimental impact on the political consciousness of liberal democracies after World War I by encouraging their unwarranted confidence in disarmament and international law as the basis of world peace.

The indictment of idealism reached its peak in the period leading up to and immediately following World War II, with the claim that the weakening of realist statecraft aided Hitler's expansionism by encouraging an attempt to stop Nazi aggression through appeasement rather than confrontation. The idealistic approach to global security was universally repudiated after 1945, and an uncontested reliance on realism as the basis of diplomacy was rehabilitated without significant dissent.

This supposedly definitive learning experience, which put realists back in control of security policy, was encapsulated in the so-called lesson of Munich. This so-called lesson supposedly had two aspects, which are not often distinguished. First, the only way to keep the peace is by pursuing a realist course, resting security on military capability and preparedness. Second, it is dangerous to think a peaceful community can be established by disarming and adhering to law and morality in foreign policy.

These ascendant realists successfully persuaded both policymakers and the public that investing hope in a global rule of law was a complacent pipe dream producing disastrous consequences. The deemphasis on power works disastrously in a global setting, they said, because a relaxed posture by the most powerful states would inevitably tempt revisionist and expansionist states to adopt an aggressive geopolitics. The intensity of the rival globalizing ambitions of Moscow and Washington after World War II were said to confirm such a view. Anxieties about maintaining global stability in the face of this post-1945 antagonism were reinforced by the widely accepted view that the world was saved from Nazi domination only by the superior military capabilities of the Allies.

This revival of realism was further reinforced by the conviction that the Cold War was contained, preventing a third world war, only because the liberal democracies did not pursue the appeasement and isolationist policies adopted after World War I. The capacity and willingness of the West, especially the United States, to confront Soviet power with the threat of annihilation avoided war while blocking the Soviet urge to enlarge its empire.

Whereas World War I had engendered a widespread disillusionment with the war system, even on the part of the "victors," and the end of World War II gave rise to fears of apocalyptic warfare, which produced a temporary wish to get rid of atomic weaponry, the Cold War ended with a sigh of relief and a glow of self-satisfaction, based on the belief that the realist approach to global security had worked, thanks in part to the caution produced by the mutual fear of nuclear war.

There was, accordingly, no significant pressure from below or above to achieve global reform after the Berlin Wall came tumbling down in 1989. The Bush I leadership, followed by the Clinton administration, made no effort to achieve nuclear disarmament or to establish a reliable volunteer peace enforcement capability under the control of the United Nations. They instead concentrated on "growing" the world economy, primarily for the benefit of Wall Street and Davos, the most visible arenas of decision making for the main stakeholders in this new globalizing epoch of world capitalism.

In addition, any cosmopolitan conception of world order—meaning one that did not accept the Westphalian framework of realist statecraft as the basis of world order—was immediately dismissed as a species of utopianism, understood as an extreme variant of idealism. All such thinking was taken to be doubly discredited by the failure of Wilsonian internationalism and, more recently, by the Stalinist cruelties associated with "actually existing socialism." Historical facts were interpreted to vindicate Kissingerian cynicism, according to which, paradoxically, we should regard advocates of peaceful paths and global justice as *enemies* of peace and justice, while regarding prudent militarists as the best *friends* of peace. From time to time, to be sure, critical perspectives, which were always in the background, were brought sufficiently to the fore to call attention to the extraordinary risks of accidental or deliberate nuclear war as an irreversible tragedy for the human species—which was bound to happen at some point, given the error-proneness of the human species and its social practices.[9] But these occasional intrusions on the realist consensus failed to alter elite thinking.

In this Cold War climate of opinion, it was virtually impossible to get a serious hearing for progressive visions of a better world.[10] The prevalence of realism effectively closed down the political imagination, despite growing signs that ecological, economic, ethical, and political considerations were undermining Westphalian capacities to address the problems facing society or even to ensure the sustainability of advanced industrial civilization. This ideological closure, based on the dominant interpretations of the two world wars and the Cold War, persists to a large extent, reinforced in the United States by the prevailing interpretation of the great terror war as essentially a military conflict.

The Post-Westphalian World

The neoconservative version of imperial realism, while continuing the ideological closure to postrealist perspectives, did at least provide a coherent post-Westphalian option. From the point of view of morality, sustainability, and even prudence, however, it is an unacceptable option, being suppressive, oppressive, and almost certainly generative of perpetual war. It even, I have suggested, contains an inbuilt propensity toward global fascism. This neoconservative vision is, in fact, so immoral and dangerous that it has given rise to nostalgic hopes for a revival of old-fashioned realism. It is imperative, nevertheless, that the axis of security policy be shifted from realism of all types to cosmopolitan democracy, if we are ever to achieve equitable and sustainable global governance.

Another version of post-Westphalian realism is provided, of course, by the soft version of imperial realism. However, while it is ethically and prudentially preferable to the hard version, it is an incoherent approach, supposing the possibility of retaining a realist perspective in framing global policy while meeting challenges of a post-realist character. The inevitable failure of such an incoherent approach, if tried again, would likely lead to a reaction that would increase the momentum toward global fascism.

We are, in any case, at a possible turning point. The rising opposition here and abroad to both imperial state extremism and jihadist nonstate extremism is calling into question anew whether *any* version of realism is capable of underwriting a sustainable future.

This skeptical analysis of realism's capacity to provide even minimum security for the peoples of the world in this century is based on four developments of recent times:[11]

(1) the transcendence of statist relations by America's establishment of a global state, which undermines the assurance of prior realist thinking that global tyranny will be avoided by the rise of countervailing power;

(2) the emergence of a transnational political movement, animated by jihadism, that treats the world as a single battlefield, selects a series of potential targets without respect for sovereign rights or international humanitarian law, and is not restrainable by deterrence, containment, or punitive retaliation;

(3) rising threats to global environmental and social sustainability by global warming, massive poverty, pandemics, fresh water shortages, population pressure, and gross disparities of wealth and income; and

(4) the emergence of transnational social movements that adhere to a cosmopolitan program of global reform premised on nonviolence, ecological sustainability, economic fairness, human rights, and adherence to the rule of law.

Liberating the Political Imagination

These developments provide a context in which it is relevant to summon the political imagination to explore post-Westphalian alternatives to world order other than the imperialist version of realism. This summons is, in other words, to find a post-Westphalian and post-realist vision of a world order that is ethically acceptable, socially responsible, ecologically sophisticated, and politically attainable.[12] While such a vision involves a revived idealism, it differs from Wilsonian idealism by giving central attention to the question of how to make the transition from here to there. The resulting vision could, therefore, be called a "relevant utopia," which combines idealistic aspiration with careful attention to issues of necessity and practicality.

A rather drastic break with traditional ways of thinking, feeling, and acting will be needed if we are ever to establish world peace on the basis of nonviolence.

Of course, confidence in nonviolence has been alive in one way or another since the success of Gandhi in mobilizing India to achieve political independence from the British Empire without a major colonial war. Gandhi decisively demonstrated that under certain conditions, the politics of nonviolence can be effective in challenging oppressive governance. Martin Luther King Jr.'s leadership of the civil rights movement in this country further confirmed the political potency of nonviolence within a given historical setting.

However, in spite of these and other dramatic demonstrations of the efficacy of nonviolent tactics, the basic political consciousness, especially among elites, has continued to be shaped by the belief that only violence can either keep the peace or produce change. The willingness to wage war and engage in the preparation for war is still overwhelmingly thought to provide the only practical, if admittedly precarious, approach to world peace.

Since 9/11, the debate in America about peace and world order has been radicalized. On the one side, 9/11 reinforced the tragic view that there is no genuine alternative to war as the basis of global security. This is certainly the way in which the Bush-Cheney administration has responded, and this response has been fully endorsed, moreover, by the nominally independent media and even by the elected representatives of the opposition party.

Increasingly, however, some slight receptivity to alternative ways of grounding world order is arising, especially in light of the administration's insistence of embarking upon an imprudent war of choice against Iraq. This war has been interpreted in many places as in effect a unilateral declaration of war against all forces hostile to Washington, as well as clear evidence that the "anti-terror" campaign is largely a ruse to mobilize support for the hard option of global empire. Alternative thinking is being articulated by unexpected voices.

In February 2003, the prime minister of Malaysia, Mohamad Mahathir, welcoming a meeting of the Non-Aligned Movement to Kuala Lumpur, delivered a rather remarkable speech. My affirmation of Mahathir's antiwar presentation does not, of course, imply an endorsement of his provocative statements in the same speech about the overwhelming Jewish influence in the world or of his authoritarian rule of Malaysia. Citing Mahathir's depiction of the menace of war to the human future is analogous to quoting from poems by Ezra Pound, valuing him sufficiently as a poet to quote him in spite of his pro-Fascist political rants.

The Mahathir antiwar, anti-Western perspective, clearly rooted in the distinctive unfolding of world politics after 9/11, is certainly one of the most constructive visionary speeches on the subject of world order given by any political leader in recent decades. Only Mikhail Gorbachev in the mid-1980s spoke in this imaginative way about the need for drastic global reform. Not since Woodrow Wilson's efforts to transcend the war system after World War I has there been such a sustained critique of war by a head of state. The fact that such a vision was articulated at a gathering of the Non-Aligned Movement, which has at various times been an important source of pressure for a more equitable world order, is certainly significant. The tenor of Mahathir's outlook can be conveyed by quoting a couple of passages from his significant effort to think outside the box:

> September 11th has demonstrated to the world that acts of terror, even by a
> dozen people, can destabilize the world completely, put fear into the hearts

of everyone, make them afraid of their own shadows. But their acts have also removed all the restraint in the countries of the north. They now no longer respect borders, international laws, or even simple moral values. They are now talking of wars and the use of military conquests in order to change governments. They are even talking of using nuclear weapons. It is no longer a war against terrorism. It is in fact a war to dominate the world, the chromatically different world. [Mahathir seems to mean here the white world trying to govern the nonwhite world.] We are now being accused of harboring terrorists, of being axis of evil countries. The non-aligned movement has a lot of problems, issues that it must tackle, but at the moment the most important threat we face is the tendency of the powerful to wage war when faced with opposition to the spread of their dominance. We cannot fight a war with them. Fortunately, many of their people are also sick of war. They have come out in their millions to protest the warlike policies of their leaders. We must join them, we must join their struggle with all the moral force that we can command. War must be outlawed. That will have to be our struggle for now. We must struggle for justice and freedom from oppression from economic hegemony. But we must remove the threat of war first. With this sword of Damocles hanging over our heads, we can never succeed in advancing the interests of our country.[13]

Mahathir was hence proposing a radical shift in the third world's agenda that is sensitive to the way in which the geopolitics of domination is being sustained by war.

He went on to make a specific recommendation, namely, that the Non-Aligned Movement should support a policy incorporated into the Japanese constitution after World War II: "When Japan was defeated, it was allowed to spend only 1 percent of its GDP on its armed forces. If such a condition can be imposed on Japan, why can it not be imposed on all countries?" This proposal was reportedly greeted with wildly sustained applause from the assembled delegates. Such an initiative would immediately free needed resources to deal with many of the problems of poverty, the environment, and of disease that are causing severe harm all over the world. Savings of hundreds of billions of dollars annually would result, enabling the reallocation of resources to pressing societal needs.

Adoption of this policy by any country would also involve a promising move away from realist thinking and the war system, a move that would challenge other countries to follow suit. Additionally, it would be an inspiring and mobilizing development from the perspective of oppositional politics in democratic societies and in relation to the perspectives of global civil society.

Mahathir made a further point that illuminates the way in which fundamental change by the powerless comes about in the political realm:

We know we are weak, but we also know we have allies in the North. They too want the abolition of war, the slaughter of people for whatever reason. They may not agree with us on every point, but in the opposition to war, very many will be with us. They are ready to oppose their warlike leaders. We must work with them. This then is our struggle. We are not irrelevant. We are not anachronistic. We have a vision, a vision to build a new world order, a world order that is more equitable, more just, a world order which above all is free from the age-old belief that killing people is right, that it can solve problems of relations between nations.

I give Mahathir's speech this attention because his message addresses the war system with critical verve and is creatively responsive to what I have been diagnosing as a severe world order crisis. What he is advocating includes an awareness of the starkness of the choices that face humanity at this stage of history. He sees that no mere moderation of the policies by the United States and other leading countries can produce an acceptable series of world order adjustments and that if imperial governance is to be challenged, the challenge must take the form of a radical attack on the role of violence as the foundation of global security and the maintenance of the inequality of material conditions. Mahathir also recognizes the globalizing dynamic of the war system, which makes it impossible for a sovereign state to opt out of the system on its own or even to escape its harmful effects without collaborating with antiwar elements in other countries, especially the United States, the headquarters of the global empire.

I also want to mention a text authored by Jonathan Schell, a writer, famous for *The Fate of the Earth*, who has consistently and eloquently expressed moral concern about the politics of our times. A more recent book by him, *The Unconquerable World*, is an indispensable contribution to post-realist thinking.[14] If its argument were to be widely accepted, it could produce, in due course, a solution to our world order crisis. Writing as an accomplished student of world affairs who is fully cognizant of realist arguments and the failures of past schemes for global reform, Schell offers us a comprehensive assessment of the underappreciated historical role of nonviolent strategies of change and of the complementary futility of relying on war to achieve global security. Like Mahathir, Schell believes that war has become an increasingly irrational means to achieve policy goals, including security.

Although Schell is a determined opponent of the menace of American imperialism, he focuses primarily on the technological menace involved in modern war. For Schell, political realism has become increasingly unrealistic because the technology of mass destruction overwhelms the means/end calculus associated with the rationality of war. The seriousness of this situation, which has existed for several decades, is now aggravated by the extraordinary vulnerability of conventionally powerful states to devastating attacks on population centers that a few dedicated individuals willing to martyr themselves can inflict. There are many scenarios: attacking nuclear facilities, repeating a spectacle of devastation on the scale of 9/11, disrupting essential infrastructure of cities, disabling major cyber networks. Schell underlines this pervasive vulnerability of modern states, for which there is no reliable defense. Efforts to achieve a high degree of vigilance impose a huge price, both economic and normative, including the abandonment of basic precepts of a free society.

Schell also explains how some of the most dramatic social changes in the past have come about without a primary reliance on violent politics. He shows, for instance, that the transformations associated with the French Revolution and the Russian Revolution were brought about largely without sustained violence of any kind. More recently, the Iranian revolution achieved success largely by the mobilization of society to mount an overwhelming display of peaceful opposition and resolve.

The unlearned lesson of Vietnam is that although an army can defeat an army, it cannot defeat a people. We may hope that this lesson is relearned, however painfully and partially, from the anguishing American occupation of Iraq. This kind of piecemeal, on-the-job learning tends, however, to be superficial, limited to context, hidden beneath rationalizations for a failing policy, and soon forgotten or suppressed by new leaders with geopolitical ambitions and realist attacks. Every president since 1975 has appealed to the American people to reject the "Vietnam syndrome," which was allegedly causing the United States to pursue a timid foreign policy inconsistent with its national interests.

But this learning about the dysfunctionality of war is not sufficiently deep to overcome the addiction to violence embedded in structures of behavior and thought, especially those of the power wielders of world order. This embeddedness, consistently reinforced by media and state propaganda, continues to make citizens resistant to repudiations of war, despite the mounting evidence of its dysfunctionality. Such resistance is at its height in America, where entrenched interests daily nurture the perception of war as indispensable for security and global leadership.

Schell is also sensitive to changes in the 1990s suggestive of a growing transnational movement for global justice. For example, the international community has, for the first time, opposed genocidal behavior within particular societies by means of intervention, overriding sovereign rights. Despite the moral rationale for humanitarian intervention, suspicions accompanied such diplomacy, partly because it seemed highly unlikely that realist leaders would expend resources and risk national lives without possessing strategic justifications. Although this development certainly had its ambiguities, it did, in conjunction with the greater interest in the implementation of human rights standards during the 1990s, indicate a trend to subvert sovereignty if it was being relied upon to shield severe domestic abuses.

Another encouraging development was the effort to hold brutal dictators *internationally* responsible for their crimes. The attempt to extradite Augusto Pinochet, the former Chilean leader, aroused world attention after his 1998 detention in Britain. Belgium passed a law endowing its national courts with universal jurisdiction with respect to several categories of international crime, thereby stripping former leaders of their immunity from prosecution. These developments gave rise to a global grassroots movement that, in collaboration with a coalition of governments, led to the establishment in 2002 of the International Criminal Court, potentially the most important institutional innovation since the establishment of the United Nations. That such an initiative succeeded, in the face of American (and Chinese) opposition, surprised many observers of world politics.

The growth of a global justice movement was also suggested by the fact that several injustices of the past became, for the first time, concerns of the present. The dispossession of indigenous peoples and the institution of slavery were acknowledged by many governments as past "crimes" that deserved an apology and, in some instances, a program of reparations.

Another sign was the establishment of truth and reconciliation commissions all over the world, including in South Africa after the collapse of apartheid. These commissions tried in various ways to acknowledge and repudiate the crimes of the past and to give some sense of rectification to the still-living victims by ordaining that, at least, their stories would become part of the historical record. There were related efforts to recover the property and the hidden bank deposits and assets of those who had been victims of the Nazi Holocaust or Japanese imperialism.

In summary, I think it is possible to identify the beginnings of a global justice movement in the 1990s that was overall encouraging, despite some disappointing regressions (including the tragic failures to protect the Bosnians and Rwandans from genocidal behavior). Had these trends continued for another decade or so, it is likely that they would have given mainstream credibility to the existence of an alternative to imperial global governance. Their viability depended on a radically different view of order and change than that embodied in any of the versions of realism. Such a different view had to include the idea that nonviolent engagement with political activity could, in spite of realist claims to the contrary, be effective in many circumstances.

One conclusion toward which my argument has been pointing is the utmost urgency of establishing a serious and concerted pedagogy of peace within our institutions of learning.[15] We need to educate future generations of citizens with an understanding of the perils of war and the degree to which a blending of law, morality, and nonviolence can be the building blocks of humane global governance. Without the dissemination of such a post-realist understanding, it is increasingly difficult to be hopeful about the future.

In his play *Saint Joan*, George Bernard Shaw conveyed succinctly this call for new thinking. Toward the end of the play, Joan of Arc says: "Some people see things as they are and ask why. I dream of things that never were and ask why not." We need to learn to ask "why not" in a very serious way—not in a dreamy, New Age spirit, but as the basis for political renewal. Another inspirational expression of this perspective is to be found in a poem of Marwan Darwish, the great Palestinian poet: "The real path leads to the beginning of the impossible path." In other words, we will need the courage to undertake the impossible or, if that wording sounds too paradoxical, to infuse the political project of global governance with a utopian imaginary that is a call to action, not just a wish list.

Chapter 5

Democratizing the Economic Order

John B. Cobb Jr.

*I*n chapter 2, I wrote about the course of events that had been shaped by economic globalization and American imperial ambition. I noted some elements in the present situation suggesting that some redirection may now be occurring. In this chapter, I will propose new directions, but I will first survey the changes now occurring, because if we are to be at all realistic when we envision a hopeful future, we need to see what is actually happening that might provide a basis on which it would be possible to build. The first part of the chapter, then, deals with ways in which economic globalization and America's imperial reach seem to be striking some limits, and how resistance is developing in ways that may prove positive.

Growing Resistance to America's Economic Imperialism

Europe, besides being the strongest center of economy and power other than the United States, is actually growing stronger economically, while the United States is growing weaker. Although the relative value of currencies changes from day to day, overall the euro has risen substantially in comparison with the dollar. The euro may break the monopoly of the dollar as the international currency. This is a frightening prospect to an imperial power that has based much of its control on the fact that the dollar is the international currency. This change is, accordingly, a major threat to U.S. economic hegemony. Those of us who want to see multiple powers emerge, so that total domination by one nation, the United States, can be blocked, should view this as a hopeful development.

East Asia remains a center of partly independent strength. This is especially true of China and Japan, but it is relatively true of other East Asian nations as well. The United States never succeeded in crushing the national economies of East Asia in the way it crushed those of Latin America and Africa. It is true that after the debacle in the mid-1990s, it did succeed in forcing some East Asian countries to "reform," thereby giving up some of their ability to manage their own affairs. Nevertheless, their national identity as economic actors has not been weakened to the extent that this has occurred in Africa and Latin America. They still retain some autonomy.

"Reform," incidentally, is an interesting word to use in this respect. In the not too distant past, it suggested a move in a more democratic and egalitarian direction. Today, "reform" means abandoning programs favorable to the poor in favor of those that benefit international capital, making national assets available for purchase by that capital, and lowering standards for labor and the environment so as to become more competitive in the global marketplace.

The deep suspicions and animosities felt by both Koreans and Chinese toward Japan have made it easy for the United States to deal directly and separately with these countries. When the ancient animosities are roused, the observer sometimes suspects American manipulation. In spite of frequent setbacks, however, East Asian countries have recently been showing signs of working together. Already Japan's trade with China exceeds its trade with the United States. If these countries brought their national economies into a relationship remotely similar to that of Europe, East Asia would become a center of economic power as strong as Europe and with greater prospects of further growth. Economic power gives rise to political power. East Asia would not be subject to control by the United States.

At present, moves toward cooperation are limited to the economic sphere. Political integration is not even being considered. However, if Europe was able to overcome the legacy of centuries of national rivalries and mutual suspicion, it is not impossible that East Asia could move in that direction. Of course, the United States is doing everything it can to work with these countries individually and to discourage them from making the moves they might make collectively. But the development of an East Asia bloc, which could challenge American hegemony there, is not impossible.

In Latin America, the United States has in the past had its way with little difficulty. If somebody of whom Washington did not approve arose to take the helm in a country, there was always the possibility of assassination or of overthrow by the military. If these methods failed, the Marines could be sent in.

Recently, however, the United States has not been quite as successful in these respects. In Venezuela, it has thus far failed in its attempts to get rid of Hugo Chavez. In Ecuador and Bolivia, peasants have prevented their governments from following the dictates of the United States. The Argentines, having gone all the way with the neoliberal policies favored by Washington, only to have their economy collapse, resist a return to the subservience of the past. People in other Latin American countries have noticed what happened to Argentina and do not support agreements that would have those consequences for them. Brazil, by far the strongest nation in Latin America, elected president Luiz Inácio Lula da Silva, who had long criticized structural adjustment policies and, more generally, opposed subservience to the United States. Although all these countries move cautiously and oppose American policies only moderately, they are learning to work together. The International Monetary Fund is being forced to reshape its policies in relation to Latin America.

Implementing further free-trade agreements has become more difficult. For some time now, high on the agenda of the United States has been the creation of the Free Trade Area of the Americas (FTAA). The crucial meeting was held in 2003 in Cancun, and little progress was made. President Bush's trip to Mar del Plata, Argentina, in November of 2005 was also widely considered a failure. It is now unlikely that anything like the FTAA as initially envisioned by the United States will come into being.

The failure of regional pacts controlled by the United States may not end the advance of neoliberal policies in relation to Latin American countries. The United States will try to achieve its goals in bilateral negotiations. However, it is now possible to imagine a scenario in which Latin American nations develop greater solidarity among themselves and, on that basis, successfully limit domination by the United States.

The Middle East is another area in which the hegemony of the United States is challenged. It is true that two of the sharpest challenges, those from Afghanistan and Iraq, have been militarily destroyed. Most governments in the region try to maintain good relations with Washington. But popular sentiment is such that they cannot concede very much to the United States. If the announced goal of the United States—the promotion of democracy in the region—actually succeeded, the results might well be stronger opposition to U.S. dominance in the region. As noted in my earlier chapter, a group of these countries once led, through OPEC, a partly successful expression of independent action. Despite ancient enmities among them, there remain impulses to common action and organization not subservient to the United States.

While regional groupings show the possibility of successfully resisting the form of economic globalization associated with American imperial ambitions, the institutions created to promote this form of globalization are weakening. For more than a decade, many global nongovernmental organizations have worked to change the practices of the World Bank and the International Monetary Fund. Most of the changes actually effected have been more cosmetic than basic, but these institutions can no longer work without considering public opinion and civil society.

The greatest decline among these international institutions promoting neoliberal policies has been with the World Trade Organization. Recently, for the second time, a meeting of the World Trade Organization, this time in Miami, collapsed. The failures, in Seattle and in Miami, were primarily caused by relationships internal to the WTO, but they were also influenced by the huge demonstrations on the outside.

What is good about the collapse of the WTO? First, if an American empire is undesirable both for the people of the United States and for the world as a whole, then a weakening of American global hegemony is good. The WTO is a creature of America, which was pushing those WTO policies that generated the opposition.

A second reason for celebration is that the collapse was the result of organized resistance by third-world countries. Of course, the United States would not have been able to achieve its goals through this international organization if the policies it promoted had not been favorable to other first-world nations. With these allies, the United States had been largely successful in bringing third-world countries into line. At Miami, however, third-world nations, calling themselves the Group of 21, stood their ground and refused to make further one-sided concessions for the benefit of the first world. Coming to the meeting well prepared and well organized, for the first time they confronted the first-world nations as real participants in decision making. They did not let themselves, through individual agreements, be picked off one by one.

It is particularly interesting and encouraging that China identified itself as one of the twenty-one. China had joined the WTO only very recently. That China came quickly to see the dangers of the policies pushed by the WTO and took part in resistance to them is a major reason for viewing this event as the beginning of the end of the importance of this organization.

One may well object that there is critical need for an international organization to establish rules for trade and to press for a level playing field. No doubt there is. But the WTO was not set up for this purpose. It was set up to break down national boundaries except when these favored the first-world nations. It was set up to give priority to narrowly economic interests over social and ecological interests. Perhaps drastic change is possible, but it may be better for this organization to collapse. The real needs could be better met through an organization created by the UN General Assembly.

A Decline of Legitimacy

Thus far I have spoken of overt political and economic developments. The deeper change is one of morale and the judgment of legitimacy. These are closely related. Morale depends to a considerable degree on two convictions: first, that one is engaged in the right task and, second, that one is on the side of history. With respect to morale, there has been a deep change. I will illustrate this with the examples of Davos and Porto Alegre.

For years, the economic and political rulers of the world had gathered at Davos, Switzerland, for what they call the World Economic Forum. They came to celebrate and promote what they understood to be progress. The morale was high. They were making the world over in a way that met their needs and desires. Only in the late 1990s did they begin noticing that things were not happening the way they were supposed to happen and that protests were becoming more and more massive. Those who supported and managed the global order were finding it more difficult to find a place they could meet without being disturbed by these protests. They had to use increasing force against the protesters.

At Davos they tried to understand the objections. Some of the participants even internalized concerns of their critics. It was no longer so evident to all the global elite that economic growth trumps all other goals. They began having sessions on the problems as well as the "successes" of economic globalization. The climate and morale of the group changed. Many attendees no longer felt the excitement of being transformers of the world.

As the morale of the world elite declined, the morale of those who protested their policies rose. Since 2001, they have met, usually in Porto Alegre, Brazil, at what they call the World Social Forum. They are sure that the economic order should serve the human community rather than subordinate all else to itself. Participation in the World Social Forum has grown dramatically. Morale is high. The excitement that was once found at Davos has been transferred to Porto Alegre.

In general, participants in the World Social Forum are not persons of power. However, at least two heads of state have now taken part: Chavez of Venezuela and Lula of Brazil. Others are likely to come in the future.

Obviously, this does not mean that political or economic power has shifted from those who attend the World Economic Forum to those who go to the World Social Forum. The people at Davos still make the decisions that shape the destinies of all of us. But now they feel hemmed in by their critics, and many of them feel unsure of themselves. This is a profound, and profoundly hopeful, change.

All of this can be called a crisis of legitimacy. Those of us whose goal has been to undermine the sense of legitimacy associated with neoliberal policies and institutions rejoice in this change. The widespread recognition of the negative consequences of economic globalization and the resultant profound suspicion of the institutions created to administer it are, for many of us, signs of hope. Defenders of the economic theory that guided restructuring of the world recognize that the gains they forecast have been slow to appear and that the suffering they expected to be temporary has in fact been prolonged. They often still argue that the problem is that the theory is imperfectly embodied in the policies and that the policies have not been fully executed. They can often point to much corruption in the nations that have not prospered. In this way, despite their disappointments, many can remain true believers in their theory and continue to press for fuller compliance.

Still, this interpretation of events grows ever more difficult. The East Asian countries that retained more national control over their economies have done much better that those who went further in merging themselves into the global market. The application of neoliberal principles in the countries of the former Soviet Union has been disastrous. Most of Africa has suffered terribly as it tried to conform to the mandates of the IMF and the World Bank. The Argentinian economy was destroyed.

The legitimacy of the whole program of U.S.-dominated globalization rested on neoliberal economic theory combined with the conviction that society should serve the economy, rather than vice versa. If that theory and that conviction were sound, then reconstructing the world accordingly was objectively justified. That the required changes caused pain to some was to be expected and accepted. Much of the support for economic globalization, and even for U.S. hegemony, came from those who were persuaded of the truth of neoliberal theory and who considered economic growth to be the supreme goal of society.

As a theologian, I have considered it my role to undertake a critical examination of the economic theory underlying economic globalization and of the conviction that wealth is the supreme value. From a Christian point of view, its basic assumptions are wrong. The theory omits consideration of justice, of community, and of the natural world. The view that increasing per capita income is an efficient way of improving the human condition is mistaken. I have, frankly, been shocked at how little attention thoughtful and concerned people gave to this type of criticism for a long time. However, I have here been tracing a change. The change thus far has been primarily from acceptance to rejection of the policies implemented in the name of economic globalization. But there is also growing awareness that the theory itself is erroneous. Porto

Alegre clearly recognizes that giving primacy to economics over real human needs is wrong. The task now is not to remove distortions in the application of neoliberal economic theory but to revise the theory itself in fundamental ways. When this is done, theory will support quite different policies. The last shreds of legitimacy accorded the present order will disappear.

Will Resistance Continue to Grow?

This disappearance of legitimacy will be important. However, the global order can continue for some time without legitimacy. It has always been based in large part on the structure of global power—political, military, and economic. Alongside a few nations, especially the United States, power is now largely in the hands of enormous transnational corporations. The current global order serves them well. It also serves the imperial ambitions of the United States well. Its continuance and expansion does not end because its legitimacy is undercut. Propaganda, bribery, and force can take over much of the role that supposedly rational persuasion has played in the past.

This shift is under way. The United States has announced that if it cannot achieve its purposes through multilateral organizations, where a certain amount of persuasion is required, it intends to go it alone. This was most dramatically expressed in its policy in Iraq. In this case, the United Nations proved resistant to following the American lead and was, accordingly, bypassed. Current U.S. problems in Iraq indicate that it may have overstepped its capacities even in terms of military action. Having used blatant deceit to gain support for the invasion of Iraq and having alienated world opinion, it then had to seek assistance from the United Nations and individual nations to extricate itself from the consequences of its actions. Those of us who oppose American imperialism might view this situation as hopeful, that is, as teaching our government a lesson.

The lesson, however, has not been truly learned. The Bush administration has named as its ambassador to the United Nations a man, John Bolton, who does not believe in international deliberation and action. His intention is to "reform" this organization, and he has made it clear that the required "reform" is for the United Nations to become more fully subservient to the United States. Only if the United Nations becomes fully an instrument of American policy will it have American support.

Meanwhile, the deeper imperial and geopolitical goals of the invasion will likely be attained. The most basic purpose was to take control of Iraqi oil. The United States will probably succeed in that goal and thereby become a powerful actor within OPEC, so that OPEC will no longer be capable of autonomous action. OPEC has not actually exercised much autonomy for some time, but there will no longer be the possibility of its becoming a center of resistance. Instead OPEC oil will be largely under U.S. control.

Although the invasion of Afghanistan had international support, its deeper purposes fit with those of the Iraq war. Perhaps the most important reason for conquering Afghanistan was to gain control of the oil resources in the Caspian Sea area. When the United States controls both OPEC oil and that of the Caspian region, it will control a large percentage of the world's oil supplies. We may be sure that it will seek control over much of the remainder as well.

The desire for unilateral control of the world's oil prevents the United States from genuinely sharing responsibility with other nations. Instead, the United States may greatly enlarge its military forces through a draft. American empire building requires a much larger army than is available on a volunteer basis. Draft boards are already in place.

Politically, a draft can be implemented only in response to a new crisis situation. This could arise in many ways. One possibility is a real democratic revolt in Saudi Arabia that would install a government unwilling to work closely with American interests. Another possibility is that a minor incident could be transformed by the American press, under the tutelage of the government, into a major threat, protection from which demands great sacrifice from patriotic Americans.

In the next few decades, whoever controls the world's oil will have a very strong basis for "negotiating" with other countries. Oil production is at or near its peak while demand continues to grow. Rational persuasion may not be needed to bring countries into line. Those nations that have resisted U.S. domination thus far may abandon resistance to American imperialism if their choice is between having oil to run their transportation, agribusiness, and industries and resisting American hegemony in the economic and political spheres.

My point is that we cannot assume that resistance to American domination will continue to grow. Even if American public opinion will not allow the U.S. government to use military power directly to force most other nations to do its bidding, this power can be used to gain control of oil and perhaps other strategic materials. Imperial policies may then be implemented by "negotiations." The present level of resistance may fade.

Much depends on how, as the United States moves back to bilateral negotiations, the nations with which it negotiates respond. If they abandon their now-fragile solidarity with one another, the United States will continue to expand its imperial rule economically and politically. If they strengthen their solidarity and support one another in resistance, a new world order may emerge.

I am not predicting either that resistance will grow and block American imperial ambition or that it will decline, with the world succumbing to *Pax Americana*. Both scenarios seem possible. President Bush has made clear to the world the intentions and aims of the United States. These aims are not likely to change drastically if a Democrat is elected. Only the means of realizing the goals will be moderately adjusted. No president is likely to renounce American hegemony. Will the rest of the world resist American ambitions with some unanimity, or end up competing for American favor nation by nation?

International Finance as Another Possible Check

Another way in which the imperial ambitions of the United States may be checked is through the realities of finance. Many have noted that the world is now dominated more by finance than by investments in productive facilities and trade in goods. This new form of capitalism, called "financial capitalism," is based on monetary transactions that are largely disconnected from any basis in the real economy, that is, the production and exchange of goods and services.

Money is quite mysterious. Its value—indeed, its reality as "money"—is based entirely on faith. A five-dollar bill is a useful item only because of faith. It would have no value apart from people believing that it will be accepted by other people in exchange for goods and services that do have practical value. As long as everybody shares this belief, money works. Faith is very powerful. But if people begin to lose faith in money, then inflation escalates. In the extreme case, money loses all value.

Once upon a time, money was an instrument of exchange, but money now has very little to do with exchange. The real economy—the actual production of goods and services and their exchange——is now but a small part of the total economy. Huge sums of money that are moved around the world electronically are not invested in anything concrete. They just buy up other units of money. Many students of capitalism, including its supporters, recognize that a global economic order organized around this kind of finance is precarious.

Furthermore, capitalism in general needs a growing economy in order to flourish. Markets can function in steady-state economies, but the standard forms of capitalism cannot. This is one reason that capitalist societies have in the past sought colonies and in recent times pressed for ever-increasing trade and investment opportunities. Whenever the public has been faced with a decision about expanding the market beyond national borders, supporters of the expansion have told us that failing to expand will bring the economy crashing down. This is, of course, an exaggeration. In the long run, however, the present form of capitalism may indeed, without growth, collapse.

Today it is difficult for the market to grow in a country like the United States. Those who have money to invest have few lucrative opportunities. Low interest rates are partly established by the Federal Reserve Board, but they also reflect the fact that investors have more money to lend than is sought by would-be borrowers. One reason stock prices rise so high is that the increase in their value is the major way in which capital now grows. But this, too, is based on a faith that can be undercut by events. Since underlying values do not justify the price of stocks, the market can go down as well as up, based on the mood of investors.

A major reason for the pressure by financiers on the U.S. government to demand that third-world nations privatize their economies is that this provides profitable investment opportunities. If the Free Trade Agreement of the Americas had gone into effect in the form favored by the United States, investors would be able to buy up the water resources of Latin America, its transportation facilities, and even its educational institutions and health-care delivery systems. That would be a wonderful new way to use this floating capital. If Latin Americans say, "No, thank you, we do not want to sell all that," where will the capital go?

Financial capitalism may be even more dependent on growth, and if expansion ceases, it may be seriously upset. Problems internal to financial capitalism may combine with problems generated by the increasing national debt to make it impossible for the United States to continue to fund its imperial expansion. This is especially true because of the dependence of the United States on other countries and their citizens to fund the debt. The falling value of the dollar may make investments in U.S securities less attractive to outsiders. The economic future of the United States is precarious.

How should we evaluate the prospect of such a collapse? From the point of view of the long-term prospects of the earth as a whole, it is one of the more hopeful scenarios. It is a way to end American imperial expansion. But that, too, needs to be set in a still wider context. It will slow down the suicidal human degradation of the natural environment. One reason for opposing imperial policy is that it runs counter to the global adjustments so clearly required to avoid ecological catastrophe.

The collapse of the present order is inevitable. The global economy, especially with the added burden of enormous use of resources for military purposes, is radically unsustainable. It is rapidly exhausting the earth's resources and polluting the environment. Its effects on the climate and weather patterns are still unpredictable in detail, but all the likely scenarios are frightening. Humanity does not have a century to reorder its affairs. Unless the present course of development is derailed fairly soon, the resulting ecological collapse will be far more terrible than a financial collapse.

A financial collapse in the United States would cause great disruption of tens of millions of lives and considerable human suffering. People like myself, whose income is totally based on present financial structures, would have acute difficulties. The collapse *could* lead to totalitarian government, not a pleasant prospect. Nevertheless, if we consider the various scenarios of how the present order may end, a financial collapse appears to be one of the least destructive forms.

In this regard, developments in Argentina are instructive and basically encouraging. That country has gone through a financial collapse and has survived. It survives because the real economy is still there. The farms are still producing food, the cattle are still out there on the range, the factories are still there, the raw materials are still there. The people are finding ways to make the real economy function despite the collapse of the money economy. At least for a while, many factories that were closed for financial reasons still produced badly needed goods because they were operated mostly by the workers. The people found new ways to make the real economy function so that they could survive.

The situation in Argentina has, it must be emphasized, been extremely difficult and even dangerous. The transition the Argentine people have been forced to go through has been a painful one. The problems that lie ahead are daunting. But the collapse of the financial economy has not led to massive starvation or loss of other necessities. A financial collapse internationally and in the United States could be the occasion for reconstructing the world on different lines without the massive suffering involved in an ecological collapse. It could give the world time to postpone and mitigate the ecological crisis and even, perhaps, to reduce its virulence.

All of this is to say that we may be at a point at which proposing different ways of organizing our society is not irrelevant fantasy. If there is financial collapse, or if resistance to present globalizing and imperial policies becomes stronger, new patterns will have to be attempted. I have described some of the developments in global affairs on which a new world order might build. But they do not assure what direction would actually be taken if the present global economy and American imperialism end.

What Kind of New World Order Do We Want?

What kind of a world would we like to see come into being out of the current situation? I will offer my proposals under two headings. (1) Economism, which is the subordination of all other values to economic growth, should end. The economy should serve society. (2) The principle of subsidiarity should be implemented. That is, decisions should be made at the lowest practicable level.

The End of Economism

We want a world in which the economy is in the service of society. We should not have society in the service of the economy. Economism, which has been the dominant religion of the world for fifty years, has viewed society as serving the economy. It is not only business and financial institutions that serve the economy. Education from preschool through graduate school is now organized in the service of the economy. Increasingly, even the legal system is asked to serve the economy. Congress serves the economy, as does the administration.

In this country, we have gotten used to this hierarchy of values. It no longer even seems strange to us that institutions of higher education exist to serve the economy. But not many years ago, people assumed that higher education was to prepare leaders for society and to transmit and develop our cultural inheritance. The idea that the main task of educational institutions is to serve economic growth involves a profound cultural change into which we have all been sucked. It is morally wrong; it is socially wrong; it is humanly wrong.

This idolatry of economic growth is wrong for the economy as well. The economy, to function well, depends on cultural values that it does not inculcate and even erodes. The individualism it fosters works against the team spirit it needs from its workers. The selfishness to which it appeals to make the system work leads to exploitation of corporations by their CEOs rather than to the honesty and loyalty required for healthy corporations.

A society in which the economy will function to realize human and ecological goals chosen by the broader society, reversing the subordination of social, human, and ecological values to economic values, is not difficult to conceive. Societies that have not succumbed to economism still exist. Even our close neighbors, the Canadians, and our close relatives, the Europeans, give far more attention to noneconomic values than do we. We can certainly imagine an even fuller reversal. But it may be hard to see how we get from here to there.

We have noticed the name under which people gather annually at Porto Alegre: the World *Social* Forum. They thereby contrast their commitments with those of the elite who gather at Davos in the World *Economic* Forum. At Porto Alegre, people understand that the economy should again be embedded in society. It is highly desirable that this happen at a national level. Democratic decisions expressing the deepest values of the people can shape legislation that will channel economic activity in ways that move toward the achievement of these values. This would be a great gain. But changes are needed at other levels as well.

Consider what now happens in our economistic system. When Boeing threatens to leave the state of Washington, what is the response? Political leaders of various cities and states that are interested in attracting Boeing compete with each other in offering tax concessions and direct subsidies. Since corporations can move their production around the country quite freely, they are in strong position to bargain with political leaders who want to provide jobs for their people. The political order has to make these gifts to corporations in order to survive.

Globally, the situation is much worse. What happens is often described as the "race to the bottom." Once national economies have been destroyed for the sake of economic globalization, political leaders must compete for investments. This competition is to offer the cheapest labor, the lowest workplace standards, the most docile workforce, and the fewest environmental restrictions.

Competition among governments for investment, both within the United States and in the world as a whole, indicates the difficulty of ending economism without localizing economic activity. Only with economic decentralization can the ideals of subsidiarity be realized.

Implementing the Principle of Subsidiarity

We suggested above that there is some trend to developing multiple centers of power around the world. This trend could function to counter American imperial ambition. There is no assurance that such regional blocs will function democratically within themselves, although the European model provides hope. There is also no assurance that they will work with each other to develop stronger and more democratic global institutions. But there are hopeful indications that in much of the world the recognition of the need for global institutions representative of the people of the world is stronger than in the United States. It is not unreasonable to hope that regional blocs will cooperate effectively with one another and grant significant authority to institutions devoted to the well-being of the planet as a whole.

The structure that is foreseeable along these lines would still be a long way from the full global democracy that David Griffin writes about. However, if in a global legislative body an African bloc, a Middle Eastern bloc, a South Asian bloc, a Far Eastern bloc, and a Latin American bloc had power more or less equal to that of the European Community or the United States, that would be a major step in the direction of global democracy. A global body of this sort could decide on what further steps to take.

The principle of subsidiarity is fully compatible with strong global governance to deal with global problems. It calls for adequate regional governance to deal with regional problems, and adequate national governance to deal with national problems. But the decentralization for which it calls goes much further. It calls for decentralization of power within nations as well. Such power is both political and economic, and significant political decentralization requires economic decentralization as well.

The goal is for local areas to become able to meet their own necessities, starting with food. The idea of "food first" has been around a long time and has always been the right idea. Those who want a global economy have ridiculed the goal of local self-sufficiency, because they believe it to be more efficient for each locale to produce whatever it produces best, export its surplus, and buy from other places what can be grown there more cheaply. That is the logic of the global market. For the rich, this market provides a vast variety of produce at low prices. But it does so at great cost to principles of sustainability and to the health and security of local communities. In addition to the ecological costs, going global disempowers local people. If people in local areas can sustain themselves in food and other necessities, it is possible for them to aim at the control of their own economy. They can continue to trade, especially in luxuries, but they are free to trade or not to trade. The terms of trade set by outsiders no long control them.

The supporters of dominant current trends have also ridiculed the family farm as the means of producing food. For them, the economies of size achieved by industrialized monoculture farms point the way of the future. But the evidence in their favor is modest. Certainly agribusiness produces a great deal of food and distributes it throughout the globe. But the cost to the land and in the use of scarce resources is very high. Present practices, heavily dependent on petroleum and natural gas, are unsustainable. Meanwhile, those who have maintained more traditional family farms, like the Amish, have continued to flourish through the years and will be far less disturbed by the now-imminent oil crisis. They give the lie to the idea that only highly mechanized agriculture can succeed. Those family farms that are now moving toward organic production will also do well.

The contrast between being part of a larger trading system and becoming a local economy has been illustrated recently in Cuba. Its recent history is encouraging. Cuba had developed an economy that, from the point of view of the ideal of subsidiarity, was as bad as a capitalist economy. Much of the land was taken over by the government, which used huge farms with gasoline-dependent machinery to raise sugar for export. It used oil also for insecticides, herbicides, and fertilizers as well as processing and transportation. This whole economy was based on exporting sugar to the Soviet Union and importing oil and foodstuffs in return. Obviously this arrangement gave the Soviet Union both economic and political control over Cuba. As soon as the Soviet Union collapsed and these trade relations ended, the huge state-owned farms became inoperable. They had been organized for one purpose: producing sugar for export. The sugar could not be consumed in Cuba and, in any case, the gasoline was not available to run the machinery.

Because of the American blockade, Cuba was forced to develop self-sufficiency in necessities, especially food. It had to do so without oil and oil products, a challenge to which the large, state-run farms proved unable to respond. Cubans suffered immensely from food shortages and, indeed, shortages of all kinds. Nevertheless, the transition was made without massive starvation or social breakdown. Fortunately, alongside the large state-controlled farms were numerous small, privately owned ones. These proved able to shift to organic food production quite rapidly. In cities, moreover, it proved possible for many families to grow considerable amounts of food. Cuba now has a sustainable agriculture, which feeds its people. It has moved a long way toward a self-sufficient economy.

I am not holding up Cuba for its moral virtue. It did not choose to become self-sufficient in food or to grow it organically. It was forced to do so by the collapse of the Soviet Union combined with a cruel blockade by the United States. The alternative was starvation. Nevertheless, once it turned to the new agriculture, it recognized its desirability. Even if the blockade is lifted, I doubt that Cuba will voluntarily go back to the kind of agriculture it had before. This will happen only if it is forced to enter the global market, redevelop an export-driven economy, and sell its land to agribusiness.

We have here an example of a country that in a period of four or five years made the transition from being a part of a trade economy to being a self-sufficient food producer, meeting its own needs without oil. In doing this, it has greatly reduced its contribution to climate change and the exhaustion of its own soils. It is not vulnerable to becoming a part of the American empire simply because of its economic needs, such as need for the oil controlled by the United States. In this way it provides a model for the rest of the world. Of course, this does not guarantee freedom, since military invasion remains possible, and Cuba's proximity to the United States makes this threat especially critical. Nevertheless, Cuba has shown that small countries can retain considerable political freedom if they can take care of their own basic economic needs. Cuba proves that decentralization and disconnection from the trade economy is possible. Cuba proves that whereas the global economy inevitably depends on oil, a decentralized economy need not. A world composed of numerous relatively self-sufficient regions, based on organic agriculture, could provide a decent life for the people of the globe on a sustainable basis.

The hope must be that the transition to local economic autonomy, and especially to the organic production of agricultural products, can take place in most places under more favorable circumstances. A longer transition, with continuing opportunities for trade when needed, would cause far less dislocation and suffering than Cuba experienced. But Cuba's success in peculiarly difficult circumstances stands as a beacon of hope.

A Community of Communities of Communities

Huge regional blocs, nations, and small localities are all important units in a more sustainable, more democratic, world. But they do not suffice. The model of subsidiarity is that of a community of communities of communities. If each local area cut off its relations with others and had nonsupportive relationships with its neighbors, the result would be a form of anarchy and chaos that would be just as bad as having everything controlled from the top. The goal is to find a way between the two extremes of anarchy and top-down, total control. The image of a community of communities of communities is the most promising alternative model. Everything should be done at the lowest level at which it can be done. That is where the control should lie. Reordering society, and especially the economy, so that more decisions can be made locally is part of the solution.

Today, however, there are numerous critical problems that can be dealt with only in larger geographical areas. Much of the economy must be organized at these larger levels. In the United States, counties might count as the local units, but much industrial production will have to be at the state level and some at the national level. The larger nations should decentralize their economies and their political decision making, on the one hand, while giving some of their decision-making power over to regional blocs, on the other. Yet they, too, should remain important levels of political and economic life.

At the same time, more and more of the issues humanity faces are global and can be dealt with only at the global level. The regional blocs would need to develop institutions for global governance that had the authority to enforce their decisions. Without far more power in the hands of global political institutions, humanity will not survive the crises that lie ahead.

This is why, even though Griffin and I have somewhat different sensibili-
ties about these matters, I celebrate his advocacy of global democracy. We
must have strong centralized global government, but with as much decentralization of both political and economic power as is possible. I begin with the
principle of subsidiarity and recognize the need for centralized decision making about the fate of the earth and enough power to enforce decisions. He
begins with the urgency of establishing a democratic global order and recognizes that it must have a federal character. Our approaches remain fundamentally complementary. We strongly agree that the domination of the world
by one superpower is the profoundly wrong way to attain global order.

Chapter 6

Global Empire or Global Democracy: The Present Choice

David Ray Griffin

*I*n chapter 1, I argued that the American empire did not come about accidentally. In this chapter, I begin by suggesting that it is also not accidental that an
empire of global scope has emerged. I then make three more points: that it is
not accidental that this global empire is not benign; that the best way to overcome this empire would be through the creation of a global democratic government; and that the creation of such a government may be possible. All these
points are in support of the chapter's overall thesis, that the question before
us now is not *whether* we will have global governance but only *what kind*—
whether it will be exercised by an imperial power or by democratically chosen leaders.

The Non-Accidental Emergence of a Global Empire

The emergence of an empire of global scope, far from being an accident of
history, has been a probability ever since the emergence of civilization and
the war system. Why this is so is explained in *The Parable of the Tribes* by
Andrew Bard Schmookler, whose argument I will summarize.[1]

The War System

The war system originated within the past ten to twelve thousand years.
This origination was closely related to the rise of civilization, with its cities
and agriculture. Prior to this, when people lived in small tribes that supported
themselves by hunting and gathering, violence between tribes certainly
occurred. Desires of revenge and other motives would have led tribes to carry
out savage raids on each other from time to time. But the hunting-and-gathering
mode of existence would have provided no motive for a war system as such.

For example, they had no incentive to take slaves, because captives could not have been given enough freedom to share in the hunt, so they would have simply provided more mouths to feed.

But the rise of civilization changed all this. Slaves could be assigned the drudge work involved in agriculture and the building of walls and water canals. Women captives, besides working in the homes and the fields, could bear children to build up the city's defensive and offensive capacity. The cities, with their cultivated lands and their domesticated herds, provided additional motives for attack. The rise of civilization brought the institution of war.

Once the war system began, every tribe was forced to participate. Even if most societies wanted to be peaceful, any one society could force the rest to prepare for war or risk being subjugated or annihilated.[2] In Schmookler's words: "Nice guys are finished first."[3]

The State of Anarchy

Schmookler's perspective in many respects follows the classic analysis provided in the seventeenth century by Thomas Hobbes, which became the basis for the dominant approach to international relations, called political realism. According to the Hobbesian-realist analysis, the interstate realm is a state of *anarchy*. This term is used not in its popular sense, to mean a totally chaotic situation, but in its technical sense, to mean simply the absence of a superior power to regulate the behavior of the states to each other, perhaps by declaring and enforcing moral norms. The resulting fact, that states must therefore rely entirely on themselves, is regarded as the key to understanding international relations. As summarized by the editors of a volume entitled *The Perils of Anarchy*, "realists regard anarchy—the absence of any common sovereign—as the distinguishing feature of international life. Without a central authority to enforce agreements or to guarantee security, states must rely on their own means to protect their interests."[4]

In this anarchical situation, it is simply power—not power qualified by moral principles—that determines the relations between the tribes. As David Held puts it, "Realism posits that the system of sovereign states is inescapably anarchic in character; and that this anarchy forces all states, in the inevitable absence of any supreme arbiter to enforce moral behaviour and agreed international codes, to pursue power politics in order to attain their vital interests."[5] The classic formulation was provided by Thucydides, who has the Athenian general give other peoples no choice except whether to be taken over peacefully or violently—adding that if they had the superior power, they would do the same to the Athenians.

Anarchy, according to this Hobbesian-realist analysis, means the war of all against all. The point is not that you actually fight against everyone else, but that every other society is at least potentially your enemy. War, accordingly, is brought on not only by the desire of one society's leaders for additional power, riches, and glory. It can be brought on simply by one society's fear that another society is amassing military power to attack it. Thucydides again provides the classic statement, having his general say, "If we cease to rule others, we are in danger of being ruled ourselves."[6]

Kenneth Waltz, the leading developer of the school of thought known as neorealism, says that although there are many causes of war, anarchy is fundamental, because it is the "permissive cause"—the one that allows almost anything else to become an immediate cause of war.[7]

I should add here that although Waltz's analysis is essentially correct, Hidemi Suganami, in a book called *On the Causes of War*,[8] has shown that Waltz's claim needs a slight qualification. As Suganami points out, anarchy is not the only permissive cause of war. Two other permissive causes are equally fundamental: humanity's capacity for violence and humanity's inclination to live in societies. This correction does not, however, undermine the implication of Waltz's analysis, since those features of human life cannot be overcome. Waltz's analysis merely needs to be revised to say that international anarchy is *the permissive cause of war that could be eliminated*.

The Endless Spiral of the Capacity for Violence

The next point of Schmookler's analysis is that in the present anarchical state of civilization, the power to exert violence inevitably grows. A new offensive weapon created by one tribe forces the other tribes to create new defenses. These defensive advances then lead competing tribes to develop new offensive weapons, and so on. Likewise, each advance by any one tribe will soon spread to the other tribes within striking distance. Once this occurs, the advance no longer gives the first tribe an advantage, so it is impelled to develop still more deadly weapons.

Furthermore, a move that may be intended defensively will often look offensive to others, evoking further efforts by them to increase *their* capacity for violence.[9] This dynamic is known as "the security dilemma," because every time a state does something of this nature to make itself more secure, it ends up being less secure.[10]

There is, moreover, no stopping point in this spiral. In Schmookler's words, "there can be no end point in the maximization of power."[11] The truth of

Schmookler's position is supported by the fact that even the creation of nuclear weapons, the seemingly ultimate weapons, did not slow down the drive to invent more weapons to get an edge over potential enemies, as shown by the twin drives to invent "smart weapons" and to weaponize space.

The Way Out

Convinced that this process will lead to self-destruction sooner or later, Schmookler argues that the only solution is to overcome global anarchy by creating a government at the global level.[12] In holding this view, Schmookler is not alone. In *The Pursuit of Power*, William H. McNeill, one of our major historians, provides support not only for Schmookler's assessment of the importance of the war system in shaping the direction of civilization, but also for Schmookler's view as to the only way out. McNeill says, "To halt the arms race, political change appears to be necessary. Nothing less radical than [a global sovereign power] seems in the least likely to suffice. . . . The alternative appears to be sudden and total annihilation of the human species."[13]

In saying that global government is the only way to overcome the war system, Schmookler and McNeill are simply taking the Hobbesian analysis, on which political realism is based, to its logical conclusion.

Hobbes himself, to be sure, did not draw this conclusion. He argued that although anarchy at the international level is a threat to our security, it is not nearly as threatening as anarchy *within* our country would be. He argued, therefore, that although domestic anarchy led people to surrender their freedom to an all-powerful state—which he called "Leviathan"—in exchange for security, the international anarchy was not sufficiently threatening to lead people to create a state at the global level. Hobbes's argument has, furthermore, been repeated by many of the most prominent realists, such as Kenneth Waltz (even though he agrees that a world government would provide the only way to put an end to warfare).[14] It is generally thought, therefore, that political realism as such rejects the idea of global government.

However, David Gauthier, after a careful analysis of "the logic of Leviathan," argues that in today's world, Hobbes would consider global government necessary, because the creation of nuclear weapons has made the international anarchy as threatening to our security as local anarchy would be.[15] There are, furthermore, several other realists who have argued that international anarchy, combined with modern weapons, requires global government to prevent civilization's self-destruction. This argument, formulated most famously in Lowes Dickenson's 1926 book, *The International Anarchy*,[16] has been stated by many others since.[17]

The Alternatives We Face

The relevance of this analysis to imperialism is that the state of anarchy, in being the permissive cause of the war system, is thereby the permissive cause of empires.[18] Realist James Speer, having said that anarchy "is the principal variable in explaining international conflict," adds, "[Anarchy] is innate in the nature of all international systems, up to the point at which they may disappear into empires."[19] In other words, with the emergence of an empire, anarchy is overcome, at least temporarily, because the imperial power becomes a de facto government over all the lesser powers.

This development has, of course, occurred many times, in various regions of the world. But prior to our time, all empires have been merely regional, so that the planet as a whole was still in a state of anarchy. In our time, however, the logic of the parable of the tribes has resulted in technologies of global reach, so that a global empire is now possible. Indeed, it is also already largely a reality. Insofar as the American empire becomes fully inclusive, global anarchy will be overcome.

Indeed, some proponents of the American empire are advocating it precisely on these grounds. In the first chapter, I quoted Richard Perle's 2003 statement that because the United Nations has failed to overcome anarchy, the world needs the kind of order that only the United States can provide.[20] Charles Krauthammer had made a similar point back in 1990, just after the collapse of the Soviet Union turned the bipolar world into what he called "The Unipolar Moment," in which the United States should be "unashamedly laying down the rules of world order" and "enforc[ing] them." Pointing out that the United Nations can guarantee nothing, Krauthammer said, "The alternative to unipolarity is chaos."[21] In 2003, Lawrence Kaplan and William Kristol wrote, "The alternative to American leadership is a chaotic, Hobbesian world," in which "there is no authority to thwart aggression, ensure peace and security or enforce international norms."[22]

What Perle, Krauthammer, Kaplan, and Kristol fail to point out, of course, is that although this brave new world of global empire will indeed be post-Hobbesian, there will still be "no authority to thwart aggression" *from* the United States and no one to "enforce international norms" *upon* the United States. These advocates of an American empire of global scope nevertheless suggest that everyone should welcome a world ruled by America because it is a uniquely benign, even benevolent, imperial power, with Krauthammer saying, as quoted in chapter 1, that the truth of this claim is shown by America's "track record."[23] As we have seen, however, this track records shows that U.S. foreign policy has been anything but benign.

The best and perhaps only way to prevent this drive to establish a global empire by the United States—or, if the United States should fail, by some other nation or union of nations—is to replace global anarchy with global democracy.

The Non-Benign Nature of the American Empire as Not Accidental

Given global anarchy, I have said, it is not accidental that a global empire would come about sooner or later. It is also not accidental that the global empire currently in the making is not benign. We have no reason, therefore, to accept the argument that even if the track record of the United States has not been very good thus far, things have now changed, because idealists are now guiding U.S. foreign policy.

To be benign, a global empire would need to be moral, obeying such basic moral principles as "treat equals equally" and "treat human beings as ends in themselves, not as mere means." But a moral empire, while not logically impossible, would be extremely improbable.

Morality and the Ideal Observer

We can see why this is so in terms of what is usually called the "ideal observer" account of morality. According to this account, the right decision in any situation is that which an ideal observer would prefer, with an ideal observer defined as one who is *fully informed* as to all the relevant facts, *impartially sympathetic* to the feelings of all parties who would be affected by the decision, and *impartially benevolent* towards all affected parties.[24] "When we make moral judgments," says Charles Taliaferro, "we implicitly commit ourselves to hold that if there were an ideal observer . . . then the [ideal observer] would make the same judgement."[25]

Taliaferro rightly holds that the ideal observer account gives us the best account of what we mean when we say that some decision is the "right" one. The correctness of this account is implicitly supported, incidentally, by many philosophers who do not explicitly affirm the ideal-observer theory of morality. This implicit testimony comes from their emphasis on the centrality of impartiality, based on universal sympathy, to "the moral point of view." Jürgen Habermas, for example, says, "The moral point of view compels the participants to transcend the social and historical context of their particular form of life and particular community and adopt the perspective of all those possibly affected."[26] We can attain this impartial standpoint, Habermas says, "only by extending the individual participant perspective in a *universal* fashion. Each of us must be able to place himself in the situation of all those who would be affected by the performance of a problematic action or the adoption of a questionable norm."[27]

Gilbert Harman also does not explicitly endorse the ideal observer theory of morality. However, having equated "the moral point of view" with "an impartial point of view," he adds that the ideal observer theory "brings out the point that moral beliefs involve a claim of impartiality."[28] Whether explicitly or only implicitly, accordingly, the ideal observer account of morality is widely endorsed.

Besides arguably being the best account of morality, the ideal observer theory has another virtue: It provides an account of morality upon which theists and nontheists can agree. This is so because to believe in God is—or at least, we process theologians agree with Taliaferro, *should* be—to believe in the ideal observer as having not merely ideal but actual existence.

Traditional forms of theism have, to be sure, attributed to God a feature implying that God does *not* feel the creatures' feelings sympathetically—I refer here to the traditional doctrine of divine "impassibility," which says that suffering in the world evokes no suffering in God. And some traditional doctrines entail that God is *not* benevolent to all creatures—most notorious here is the doctrine that God, in creating the world, predestined some human beings to eternal punishment.

However, we process theologians, along with Taliaferro and many other philosophers and theologians, hold that the word "God" should be understood to mean *an actual being who has all the attributes of the ideal observer and no attributes that are in tension with these attributes.* Given this understanding of God, the idea that the right thing is always "what God wills" is the same as defining the right as "what an ideal observer would prefer."

Given this understanding of the meaning of morality, upon which theists and nontheists can agree, I turn to the question of why we cannot expect empires to be benign.

Why Empires Will Not Be Benign

One reason not to expect any empire to be moral is that empires are run by human beings, and we do not even remotely approximate ideal observers. Far from being fully informed about all the relevant facts needed to make decisions for the good of the world, we know only a little, primarily about our own corner of the world—indeed, primarily about our own individual lives. Far from being impartially sympathetic, we generally feel sympathy for the weal and woe of only our own bodily parts and a relatively few fellow creatures. And far from being impartially benevolent towards all fellow creatures, we seek the good primarily of ourselves and those few others whose concerns we share. It is most improbable, therefore, that the decisions of a global emperor would approximate those of an ideal observer, even remotely.

This improbability is further increased by the dynamics of states, analyzed most famously by Reinhold Niebuhr. Because of these dynamics, individuals in their role as leaders of states have even less capacity for morality, in the sense of transcendence over self-centered interests, than they do as private citizens.[29] This is partly because they have more natural sympathy for the welfare of their own citizens than they do for those of other countries, and partly because they are mandated by their job description to work solely for the good of their own citizens. The first President Bush, asked after the Earth Summit in 1992 why he refused to sign the biodiversity treaty, explained: "I am President of the United States, not president of the world and I'll do what is best to defend US interests."[30]

Still another reason for expecting any ruler of a global empire to be far from benevolent is the generalization about human nature summarized in Lord Acton's famous axiom: "Power tends to corrupt, and absolute power corrupts absolutely."[31] Acton's saying can, of course, be considered simply a secular version of the Christian doctrine of original sin, which says that all people— of all nations, all races, all genders, all classes, all religions, and all ideologies, without exception—are more or less self-centered.

From this perspective, the main heresy of Marxism was its doctrine that one class, the proletariat, was unaffected by sinful tendencies, so that it could be trusted with absolute power during a temporary "dictatorship of the proletariat." The resulting failure of many Marxist governments to build in political checks and balances lay behind their worst excesses. In the case of Stalin, for example, his possession of absolute power within the Soviet Union led to an absolutely corrupt tyranny.

The central heresy of Americanism is the conceit of American "exceptionalism," according to which being an American exempts leaders from the selfishness characteristic of leaders of other nations. Just as ideological Marxism claimed that people who belonged to, or identified with, the proletariat could be trusted with absolute power, ideological Americanism has attributed this extraordinary trustworthiness to American governments. (In my first chapter, I quoted Charles Krauthammer's assertion that although people usually recoil "at the thought of a single dominant power for fear of what it will do with its power . . . [,] America is the exception to this rule.") It is partly in the name of this heresy that American leaders are now seeking absolute power at the global level.

The wisdom behind Acton's axiom was also articulated in one of Reinhold Niebuhr's best-known statements (expressed in the language of the time): "Man's capacity for justice makes democracy possible; but man's inclination to injustice makes democracy necessary."[32] Niebuhr's first point was that because human beings have *some* capacity to adopt the moral point of view, which is the impartial point of view, human communities can rule themselves democratically.[33] But Niebuhr's second point was that because we, in spite of this capacity, have an inclination to act unjustly, democracy, with its checks and balances, is necessary. In light of this inclination—of human individuals and especially of human groups[34]—we do not dare give absolute power to any individual or any nation.

Although Niebuhr did not develop it, his analysis provides the basis for a moral-religious argument for global democratic government.

A Moral-Religious Argument for Global Democracy

Niebuhr rightly criticized Plato's idea of the philosopher-king, according to which the political ideal would be to give all power to a philosopher. Plato thought that such a king, as a lover of wisdom, could be trusted to use his power wisely, for the benefit of all his subjects. But Niebuhr, holding that "only God can perfectly combine power and goodness," argued that the expectation of an ideal king "hopes for an impossible combination of the divine and the historical."[35] On this basis, Niebuhr concluded that there will *never* be a "reign of peace."[36]

Niebuhr for the most part agreed with process theologians on the nature of God,[37] so his contrast between humans and God can be understood in terms of the contrast between humans and the ideal observer. Although God is different from the ideal observer by virtue of having *actual* existence and thereby exercising power, God otherwise has all the characteristics of the ideal observer. As omniscient, God is, like the ideal observer, fully informed about all relevant facts. As perfectly embodying receptive love, God is impartially sympathetic to all creatures. And as perfectly embodying creative or outgoing love, God is impartially benevolent to all creatures, wanting the best that is possible for them.[38]

Divine power is thereby exercised on the basis of perfect goodness, which can be attributed only to deity. Niebuhr is right, therefore, to say that only God can *perfectly* combine power and goodness.

It does not follow, however, that a world of peace, based on a high degree of justice, would be impossible. Such a world would not require a *perfect* government, only one that *approximates* the divine combination of power and goodness far more than any empire would. A global democracy could achieve such an approximation.

The global legislature as a collective body, being composed of representatives from all regions of the world, could partly make up for the defects in each individual. That is, if each representative is largely ignorant about most of the regions of the world, this ignorance could be corrected within the collective body by the knowledge of the representatives from those regions. If each representative is largely indifferent toward the welfare of peoples from most parts of the world, the sympathy possessed by the representative from these parts could make up for that indifference. The partisan biases of each representative could be balanced by the biases of the others. The global legislature could, therefore, embody firsthand knowledge of the facts, along with real sympathy for and benevolence toward the various affected parties in the various regions. Their decisions could, therefore, somewhat approximate the wishes of God or, using the other framework, the preferences of the ideal observer.

Such a government could accordingly meet the need, seen by Niebuhr, to transcend our anarchical world order, in which disputes based on conflicting perspectives are settled by brute force. "There must be an organizing centre," Niebuhr said, that can "arbitrate conflicts from a more impartial perspective than is available to any party of a given conflict."[39] If force is to be redemptive rather than destructive, Niebuhr rightly said, "it is an absolute prerequisite that it be exerted by an agency that is impartial."[40] Niebuhr in these passages did not demand perfection, only a power that is exercised with far greater impartiality than that possessed by any of the competing parties. We could hope for such impartiality from, and only from, a global democratic government.[41]

An obvious objection to this vision of how enlightened global democratic rule could be is that few if any national democratic governments have approached this ideal. This objection can be answered, however, by pointing out that all such governments have been more or less corrupted by at least two factors that would need to be ruled out in the creation of a global democracy.

These national governments have, in the first place, been corrupted by the power of money. Instead of decisions being made on the basis of the best arguments about what would best promote the common good, decisions have been made to please the selfish interests of the rich. Instead of truly being democracies, with government of, by, and for the people, these governments have in fact been plutocracies, with government of, by, and for the rich.

A second corrupting factor is that all national democracies have thus far existed within the anarchical, competitive system of states, with its "war of all against all." In this situation, the policies of a state have often been directed less at promoting the common good of its people than at protecting the existence of the state and enhancing its power vis-à-vis other states.

When these two corrupting influences are combined, gross distortions are likely, as illustrated by the enormous portion of the U.S. budget directed toward the purchase of weapons produced by corporations that have made huge political contributions. In creating a global government, nothing would be more important than instituting rigorous measures to shield it from the corrupting power of money, including all forms of bribery. Given those measures, the decisions might really be such as to promote an approximation to the general good as discerned by an ideal observer, or—as theists would say—decisions that approximate the will of God.

The Possibility of Global Democracy

Genuine global democracy would involve pan-democracy, meaning democratic governance at every level, based on the principle of "subsidiarity," according to which the authority to make decisions about some matter should be placed at the lowest level at which these decisions can be effectively made and implemented. Genuine global democracy would not, therefore, consist entirely or even primarily of democracy at the global level.

Nevertheless, its most controversial aspect has always been the idea of a government at that level, superior to the governments of the present countries. This idea has standardly been subjected to a threefold veto—that it is unnecessary, undesirable, and impossible.

The claim that it is unnecessary has become increasingly unconvincing, especially since the rise of nuclear weapons, the global ecological crisis, and the fear of a global empire.

The claim that such a government would be undesirable has usually rested on the fear that it would become tyrannical. Today, however, the question is no longer whether we will have a global government. The only question is whether it will be a democratic government, freely created by the citizens of the world, or an imperial government, imposed by one nation on the rest. And the former type is, at the very least, much less likely to become tyrannical than the latter.

There are, furthermore, many other reasons, to be mentioned below, for concluding that a global democratic government is both necessary and desirable. Answering the first two claims, however, still leaves the third one—that even if global democracy is necessary for survival and otherwise desirable, it would be impossible to create.

Of the many reasons that have been given for this claim, the most formidable one in today's world is simply the likelihood that Washington, in conjunction with its junior partners and the more general global plutocracy, would prevent it. This may well be true. It may be possible, nevertheless, to imagine a route through which global democracy might be created.

A Common Cause for Moral NGOs

We can begin imagining such a route by reflecting on the suggestion, made recently by a number of thinkers, that, in spite of America's claim to be the sole superpower, there is a second superpower: global civil society. If the people of the world were united behind a cause to which they were passionately committed, they would indeed constitute a force against which the American superpower, equipped to wage military and economic warfare, might be relatively helpless.

At the present time, however, global civil society has no such cause. A remarkable phenomenon of recent decades, to be sure, is the growth of thousands of nongovernmental organizations—NGOs—committed to moral goals. But these goals are various, with some moral NGOs working against nuclear weapons, others against war in general or some specific war, others against the weaponization of space, others for human rights, others for workers' rights, others for biodiversity, others for population control, others against global warming, others for economic democracy, others against corporate welfare, others against the IMF and the World Bank and the WTO, others for a strengthened United Nations, and so on. Some of these NGOs have joined together in what has been called the "anti-globalization movement," but for the most part each NGO focuses on its own concern, working independently or at most in conjunction with other NGOs focused on the same concern. These NGOs are usually so outfunded and outorganized by the interests they oppose that their victories are seldom and, when they do come, fleeting. Global civil society at present constitutes nothing approaching superpower status.

Global civil society could become a powerful force, however, if the majority of its moral NGOs became united behind a common cause. Global democracy could be that cause and is, in fact, the most logical candidate. Besides providing the precondition for overcoming the war-terrorism-imperialism system, it is also arguably the necessary condition for overcoming all the other problems of global scope mentioned in the previous paragraph.[42] Insofar as this argument is convincing, activists for global causes will come to realize that, *whatever their cause, it is a lost cause without global democracy.*[43] They will realize, therefore, that the practical thing to do is to work *indirectly* for their own cause by working *directly*, in conjunction with many other organizations, for global democracy. If a majority of the moral NGOs of the world join forces, combining their money, expertise, and sheer numbers, they will be able to wield tremendous influence. Out of these reflections comes a recommendation: *Moral NGOs of the world, unite! You have nothing to lose but your impotence.*

A Common Cause for the Religions

Even when combined, however, the personnel resources of the moral NGOs would be tiny compared with the giant corporations and the governments supporting them. But there is another part of global civil society that is *not* tiny—the religious traditions of the world. If we combine the adherents of Buddhism, Confucianism, Christianity, Hinduism, Islam, Judaism, Sikhism, Taoism, Zoroastrianism, and other religions, including primal religions, we have over 5 billion of the world's peoples. If a significant percentage of these religious movements and organizations became committed to the cause of global democracy, we would have a significant global movement.

But is this conceivable? Are not the religions of the world too different to join forces? Does not religious and cultural diversity prevent a common global ethic? The idea that it does has been, in fact, one of the major arguments for considering a global democratic government impossible.[44]

However, although the various religions are different from each other, some of them *radically* different,[45] they share a set of moral values. These shared moral values are, moreover, diametrically opposed to the values by which the world is now governed. The Abrahamic religions—Judaism, Christianity, and Islam—all share moral codes that entail, for example, the following injunctions:

> Do not covet your neighbors' oil.
> Do not steal your neighbors' oil.
> Do not murder your neighbors in order to steal their oil.
> Do not bear false witness against your neighbors, calling them "communists" or "terrorists," to justify stealing their oil.

The values of the present global order are equally opposed by the moral codes of Buddhism, Confucianism, Hinduism, Sikhism, Taoism, Zoroastrianism, and the various indigenous traditions.[46] They are also opposed by moral Marxism.[47]

As Hans Küng has pointed out, most if not all the traditions affirm some version of what Christians have called the golden rule—at least in its negative formulation, sometimes called the "silver rule": Do not do to others what you would not want them to do to you.[48] And yet the violation of this rule is precisely what the present world order, based on the rule of force rather than law, allows and even encourages.

A helpful way of thinking about this issue can be derived from Michael Walzer's *Thick and Thin*. In earlier writings, Walzer's concern with difference and particularity had seemed to lead him to an extreme relativism. In the debate between the "cosmopolitans," who affirm a universal morality, and the "communitarians," who emphasize the distinctive ethos of each nation or cultural tradition, he was placed totally in the latter camp, being regarded as denying any universal moral principles. In *Thick and Thin*, however, he argues that every thick, particularist morality has within it "the makings of a thin and universalist morality."[49] He now affirms, in other words, a position that can be called "communitarian cosmopolitanism" or, as Walzer would surely prefer, "cosmopolitan communitarianism."[50]

This moral position can provide the background for a federated global political system that, while affirming universal moral standards, allows for differences between the various thick traditions. This position, far from implying a homogenized world, as pure cosmopolitanism seems to do, provides a basis for *resisting* the homogenization now being ruthlessly carried out by the corporation-led "globalization."

Walzer points out that, because the world's various peoples live in terms of their own thick traditions, which are quite different from each other, the thin, universalist morality usually becomes apparent "only on special occasions," especially when there is "the sense of a common enemy."[51] In calling this universalist morality "thin," Walzer does not mean that it is unimportant. Indeed, he says:

> The opposite is more likely true: this is morality close to the bone. There isn't much that is more important than "truth" and "justice," minimally understood. The minimal demands that we make on one another are, when denied, repeated with passionate insistence. In moral discourse, thinness and intensity go together.[52]

This recognition—that we share this passionate commitment to such basic principle as truth and justice—is evoked when we become aware of a common enemy.

The common enemy of all the world's religious traditions is the present world order, with its plutocracy and imperialism based on anarchy. What we need now is only "the sense" that this is so; indeed, this sense has been rapidly forming in recent years.[53] When representatives of these various traditions look at each other in terms of their specifically theological and metaphysical beliefs, they may be convinced that their differences are more important then their commonalities. But when they look at each other in relation to the plutocratic imperialism of today's world order, they will become increasingly aware of the set of core moral beliefs they hold in common. On this basis, representatives of these traditions could fashion a "global bill of rights and duties" for a global constitution.

When we think of religion and ethics today, to be sure, we often conjure up images of religious fundamentalists wanting to impose their highly particular moral code on everyone else. The attempt to implement that desire, however, would go against one of the fundamental points of the thin morality common to all, which Walzer calls *the principle of self-determination*. It implies that people, as members of communities, have, in Walzer's words, "the basic right *to govern themselves* (in accordance with their own political ideas)—insofar as they can decently do that."[54] In other words, aside from the thin, quite abstract moral principles that the representatives at a constitutional convention would agree upon as universally valid, no other principles would be imposed on anyone. Each community would be free to govern itself in accordance with the political ideas that arise from its own tradition—with the caveat that it do so "decently." This caveat means that a global constitution should allow communities to govern themselves in terms of their own norms, as long as those norms do not violate any of the thin, universal moral principles that are included in the global bill of rights and duties by mutual consent.

We can see, therefore, that the religious passion brought by members of the various religions of the world need not undermine a common front committed to effecting a transition from today's anarchical, plutocratic, imperialist world order to a democratic world order. In this new world order, the system of settling differences by the threat and use of force would be replaced by "legal pacifism," in which disputes are settled by appeal to impartial judges. The principle of "might makes right" would be replaced by "might supporting right." The plutocrat's golden rule, according to which those with the gold make the rules, would be replaced by laws based on the religious traditions' silver rule, so that we mutually agree not to do to other people what we would not want them to do to us.

Devising laws that exemplify this silver rule would not be terribly difficult. None of us want to be persecuted for our religious beliefs, to be deprived of adequate food and water, to be arbitrarily imprisoned and tortured, to have our land or other property stolen, to have our towns and villages strafed and bombed, to have our homes demolished by tanks, or to have our family members raped or mutilated by land mines. Such a world order could, accordingly, be passionately sought by members of all religious traditions, whatever their

other differences, and regardless of whether they belong to the fundamental-
ist, conservative, liberal, or radical branch of their own tradition.

These reflections lead to the following recommendation: *Religions of the
world, unite! You have nothing to lose but your impotence.* The Abrahamic
religions—Judaism, Christianity, and Islam—are not unique in having a
vision of a form of human society that involves a "reign of God," a society
based on divine rather than demonic values. Such a vision is found in most if
not all religious traditions. But thus far, with a few temporary exceptions, such
societies have not appeared.

When religious leaders have called for the creation of a society that
reflected their tradition's principles, the "realists" have told them that they
were impractical dreamers, utopians, that only in heaven will a society based
on such principles be possible. In the world as it is, the realists have insisted,
those principles would lead to the society's destruction. And they have been
right—with regard to the world of anarchical civilization, which is the only
kind of civilization that has existed thus far. In this world, the war of all against
all requires that each society, if it is to thrive or even survive in this competitive situation, must be organized on the basis of quite different principles.

But now, with the shrinking of the world brought about by modern technologies of communication and transportation, it is finally possible to overcome this anarchical situation. By uniting to bring about a post-anarchical
civilization, the religions will have created the precondition for societies that
at least approximate their long-standing dreams of a world governed in terms
of divine rather than demonic values. Such a "reign of God" truly would be,
as it is called in John Cobb's chapter below, a "commonwealth of God,"
because the present global plutocracy, with its enormous gulf between the
obscenely rich and the miserably poor, would be replaced by a world in which
all people shared somewhat equally in the planet's resources.

Religions and Moral NGOs, Unite!

However, whereas the religions can supply great numbers of people, motivated by religious passion, to work for this cause, they will generally not have
the various kinds of theoretical knowledge and practical wisdom, based on
experience, to organize the massive global movement required to turn global
democracy, now only a vague ideal, into a concrete proposal and then a practical reality.

Some of the moral NGOs, however, do have these kinds of knowledge and
practical wisdom. They have access to massive amounts of ecological, political, economic, financial, historical, cultural, legal, and other kinds of knowl-

edge that will be needed both to make the case for a global government and to assist with the creation of an effective and acceptable constitution for it. And having long been battling with governments and corporations, they have developed various kinds of practical wisdom.

These moral NGOs will, at the same time, need some kinds of knowledge embodied in the religious traditions, such as knowledge about effecting reconciliation between erstwhile enemies and bringing about change through nonviolent means.

The complementary strengths of the religious traditions and the moral NGOs, combined with the massiveness of the project before us, suggests an inclusive motto: *Religions and moral NGOs of the world, unite! You have nothing to lose but your impotence. And you have a world to save.*

PART III   Religious Reflections
                            _____

Chapter 7

Omnipotence and Preemption

Catherine Keller

> We might be tempted to bring the whole of modern history to a tragic con-
> clusion by one final and mighty effort to overcome its frustrations. The
> political term for such an effort is "preventive war."
>
> *Reinhold Niebuhr,* The Irony of American History

*T*he explosion of 9/11 produced a vast cloud of opportunity. Some were sure
that the Middle Eastern turbulence of the end time had finally begun, the rap-
ture sure to follow. For others, "the New Pearl Harbor" provided the long-
awaited opportunity to push for a global military hegemony that could
stabilize the world. We got neither the messiah nor the stability. Instead, we
got a full-blown American empire—a phrase that at the turn of the century
still seemed like old leftist rhetoric seeking its own opportunities. At this
point, it is up to liberal and progressive religious leaders to make another use
of the "opportunity": not to proliferate homiletically overheated denunciations but to expose *theologically* the idolatry of U.S. global pretensions. These
pretensions oscillate between the military face of empire, emboldened by
9/11, and the incessant voracity of its smoother, bipartisan, economic face.
And while U.S. regimes and strategies shift, the political cloud released by
9/11 will take, it now seems, much of the new century to dissipate.

Innocence and Power

The United States does not refer to itself as an empire, since we lack a monarchy—in other words we do still have elections (more or less) and not dynas-
ties (well, not exactly). Old issues echo in the terminological question of an
"American empire." Until the Civil War, the concept of an American empire

was commonplace. George Washington and Ben Franklin routinely referred to the United States as a "rising empire." While "legend and tradition require that the American Republic appear anti-monarchical and anti-imperial," according to a historian writing half a century ago, the executive power belies this "legend of the Revolution."[1] But under the Bush II regime, our officials learned not to mince words anymore. They began to refer to our "hegemonic unipolarity" and our "appropriate global dominance." That dominance was carved into imperial marble for the twenty-first century with the declaration of our right to use overwhelming military force preemptively whenever we wish. As the earlier chapters in this volume show, the question is not *whether* America is an empire but only *what kind*.

This situation cannot simply be voted out of office. With a different administration, our global domination might be exercised with a greater sense of responsibility. But the imperial configuration will not soon dissipate. So it is time to raise theological questions about *power* and to question previous theological answers.

No great empires have been lacking in religious justifications for their apparently irresistible powers of expansion. What makes us special? Not long before his death, Edward Said stated:

> The difference between America and the classic empires of the past is that, even though each empire asserted its utter originality and its determination not to repeat the overreaching ambitions of imperial predecessors, this one does so with an astonishing affirmation of its nearly sacrosanct altruism and well-meaning innocence.[2]

Americans ask, "How can they hate *us*? Maybe we're not sophisticated like old Europe, maybe we slip up here and there (a few bad apples), but don't they see our innocent, exuberant have-a-nice-day goodness?" This aura of sacrosanct, youthful power, which has always distinguished our imperialism, requires theological decoding. A halo of unquestionability surrounds the literally boundless aggression of neoliberal economic globalization and now also our military superpower, redefined by its policy of preemptive war.

In this chapter, I should clarify, I am using the term "preemptive" war to refer to the kind of war that in international relations circles is technically called *preventive* rather than *preemptive* war. According to that usage, a *preemptive* war occurs when one country goes to war with another country upon learning that an attack from that country is imminent, with "imminent" meaning that there is no time to get the United Nations to intervene. Preemptive war in that technical sense is legal under international law. By contrast, a *pre-*

ventive war, which is illegal, occurs when one country launches a war against another country, even though there is no evidence that an attack from it is imminent, in order to prevent a *possible* attack from it sometime in the future. I find, however, that for most people—including myself—the term "preemptive" better suggests that kind of illegal war, in which the purpose is to preempt the very possibility that another country could have the wherewithal, sometime in the future, to launch an attack.[3] To make my meaning clear, I will sometimes refer to "preventive-preemptive" war.

I now return to the point that, even after our nation has declared its right to launch this kind of preventive-preemptive attack any time it sees fit, the halo of unquestionability is still largely in place. We cannot read this halo only historically or politically. It is not a mere laurel wreath, suited to a Roman god. It is alive and vibrating with theological information. Our "manifest destiny"—manifest first upon contiguous lands and then, a century ago, across the seas—has always bristled with Christian power codes. Theology may be an important inside agent in breaking codes—and also in *transcoding*: translating the codes into alternative contexts of communication. Let us try to *recode* the spiritual politics of power.

Certainly theology has an internal tradition of resistance to U.S. imperialism. Half a century ago, Reinhold Niebuhr wrote: *"[W]e have been so deluded by the concept of our innocency that we are ill prepared to deal with the temptations of power which now assail us."*[4] He thought that we had heretofore oscillated between isolationism, which means to ignore our responsibilities to other nations, and imperialism, which means "to dominate them by our power." At the dawn of the nuclear age and in the aftermath of the Second World War, the discourse of our messianic innocence was just beginning to pose its apocalyptic threat to the world. Niebuhr investigated both the Puritan and Jeffersonian sources of our delusion of innocence—a paradoxically very un-Calvinist delusion—that "we had been called out by God to create a new humanity. We were God's new Israel."[5] Niebuhr knew we would not soon forfeit our power. He called not for some new, revolutionary myth of innocence, but for a humbling sense of irony in the face of our self-contradictions.

Half a century later, still protesting our innocence, we are, if anything, even less able to discern a third way, a way of globally democratic multilateralism. In the face of our long history of domination encrypted with faith, we have failed to learn the Niebuhrian irony. Instead, we are far better armed technologically, economically, and, I fear, religiously. Absolute power is treated not as absolute corruption—not even as temptation—but as blessing.

Apocalypse and Imperial Legitimation

Hannah Arendt has argued that *violence* is instrumental and hence requires only *justification*: an end justifies the means. *Power*, by contrast, requires *legitimation*, which comes from stories of creation—of beginning and new beginning. Religion within our secular empire has provided covert legitimation: The enemy is not merely a historical foe, but a diabolical dark force against which only the white light of our messianic goodness can prevail. Over and over we have heard that "America will call evil by its name." The name of the Beast?

But religion has also offered *overt* legitimacy: We heard from President Bush in his 2002 State of the Union Address that "the liberty we prize is not America's gift to the world, it is God's gift to humanity." (So it is God's gift we have brought to Iraq.) "There's *power, wonder-working power*," our president said, "in the goodness and idealism and faith of the American people."[6] The quotation from an evangelical hymn invests our national innocence with divine power.

The irony seems to have escaped most Christian supporters of Bush: that the hymn refers to the blood of "the Lamb" slaughtered by the imperial superpower of his day. Indeed, the reference is from the most misused text of all, the book of Revelation, according to which the Beast is none other than the dominant empire of the time, Rome. The Apocalypse is a parable of terror, transcoding the blowback that brings down every human empire.[7]

It is tempting to take up a righteous apocalyptic stance of *anti*-imperialism. However, within the American context at least, the church will do better with *counter*-imperialism, along with an honest dose of Niebuhrian irony. For Christianity long ago lost its innocence, to empire itself, at the point of the Constantinian conversion of the empire to Christianity. "When the Western world accepted Christianity," wrote Alfred North Whitehead a decade after World War I, "Caesar conquered; and the received text of Western theology was edited by his lawyers. . . . The brief Galilean vision of humility flickered throughout the ages, uncertainly."[8]

Or did the loss of innocence begin earlier, even in the anti-empire of the vision of apocalypse, when it mirrors and mimics the empire—with a panorama of messianic armies, holy genocide, divine ecocide, and all-penetrating divine power? The apocalyptic codes have routinely justified empire as well as anti-empire. The Crusades were experienced as apocalypse come true—forty thousand Muslim women, children, and men were slaughtered in two days in Jerusalem. An eyewitness, rendering history as a paraphrase of Revelation 15:20, wrote rapturously of the wonderful sights to be seen: "In the Temple and porch of Solomon, men rode in blood up to their knees and bridle reins. Indeed it was a just and splendid judgment of God that this place should be filled with the blood of the unbelievers."[9]

If, as Rahul Mahajan argues, America's "War on Terrorism" has unleashed a "new crusade" with a "new rhetoric of justification," the religious code remains indispensable. As Mahajan says, "No government, whether dictatorship or democracy, can remain in power if it cannot represent its actions and ultimately its authority as legitimate."[10]

But our global hegemony has drawn its aura of sacrality not only from the warring apocalyptic extremities it provokes. We model ourselves less after the crusaders than after the British Empire. Its Protestantism was constrained and decidedly nonapocalyptic. Richard Hakluyt, a scholar writing in 1589 (at the time of Queen Elizabeth), argued that if the pope could give Ferdinand and Isabella the right to occupy "such island and lands as you may have discovered or are about to discover" outside Christendom, the English crown had a duty to enlarge and advance the faith of Christ "on behalf of Protestantism."[11] Protestantism enabled Britain to advance from mere piracy against the religiously legitimated Spanish holdings to an empire of its own. Modernity, it seems, required wave after wave of conquest for Christ.

The main problem, however, is not a past Christian loss of innocence. It is rather the persistent delusion of innocence. And yet some Christians were always waking up and "coming of age," in Bonhoeffer's sense. Christianity within its waves of influence does not only legitimate. It sometimes vehemently *withholds* legitimacy, as when Bishop de las Casas fought the brutality of his fellow Spaniards in their "New World." Or it deploys its influence for justice, as with the church-based British grassroots campaign that brought about the abolition of the slave trade in 1806.

But this evangelical achievement was not simply a work of innocence and purity: Using the same logic—that not only whites are fully human before God—the same group (the Clapham Commons group) broke through the rigid British constraint on missionary activity in India. This group did not question the British Empire but made it a tool of Christian mission—which led quite directly to a new Indian sense of cultural violation, to the Indian Army mutiny, and thereby to the barbaric British reprisals.

Such ambiguities do not *delegitimate* Christianity. They simply display its capacity for self-righteous idolatry as well as prophetic iconoclasm. It is *because* the church is implicated in empire that we can decode and transcode the idolatries of empire. Of course, the legitimating master code is not reducible to religion. It is heavily shaped by the secular rhetoric of "democracy" and "freedom" as well. But these appeals lack circumstantial credibility and, for many Americans, ultimacy. They have to be shored up by the apocalyptic, inherently antidemocratic, signals. *Legitimation* in its appeal to ultimacy is bigger than instrumental *justification.* Both are different from *explanation*, which gives reasons.

There are several likely *explanations* for the post-9/11 empire. I will list nine:

1. Plain fear, manipulated to include the Arab and the Muslim in general
2. An almost audible sigh of relief at having finally found an enemy worthy to fill the void left by the Communist Other
3. The felt virility of this identity, its explosion of potency putting behind us the longhaired Vietnam wimp-out
4. Our relation as the New Israel to the Newer or Older or Greater Israel—a state no one calls a wimp
5. The neoliberal global economy, combined with a reaction against its *dena*tionalizing tendencies[12]
6. The captivity of the U.S. media by monopoly capitalism
7. The stupefaction of the public and reduction of the U.S. attention span to the size of an ahistorical sound bite
8. The production not of engaged citizens but of docile consumers who, after bouts of apocalyptic excitement, retreat into the comfort of expensive addictions, oil foremost
9. The lack of effective cosmopolitan governance of a postmodern, ecologically interdependent globe of high-speed communications and weapons technology, producing new perils and needs—including no doubt the need for international, cosmopolitan strategies of *responsible* prevention of surprise attacks

All of these explanations are, as far as they go, true. But they do not add up to a publically persuasive justification. Together they suggest the overdetermination of our imperial condition. Legitimation is always greater than the sum of justifications. So let us direct our attention to the aura that played about all of these reasons, in a certain sense holding them together. Let us focus on *the halo surrounding our empire*, not just in its deeply embedded Judeo-Christianisms, but also in its hard-line secular state doctrine.

Evil and Idealism

How is it that we as a post-Vietnam people could come to regard military superpower, unilaterally deployed, as *good*? Not just justifiable as necessary violence, but legitimate as a virtue, a force for peace, order, and freedom? The particular justifications disintegrate—Osama, Saddam, weapons of mass destruction. Yet the glow of righteousness persists. It is not only that might *makes* right, but that this might *is* right. Manifest destiny, the special providence of America, the city on the hill, God Bless America—not to *make* us good, but because we *are* good. The phenomenon is as old as we are, and so Niebuhr's warning—that "we are still inclined to pretend that our power is exercised by a peculiarly virtuous nation"—deserves its near canonical status.

It is perhaps not surprising, therefore, that this very sentence gets attacked in *The War over Iraq*, a book written to prepare the way for war *with* Iraq. The authors, Lawrence Kaplan and William Kristol of the Project for the New American Century, (rightly) accuse Niebuhr and the political realists in general of trying to inhibit "a messianic impulse" that was, in their view, able to "lead America to upset the balance of power between it and the Soviet Union." At *this* point, they argue, "there is something perverse in continuing to doubt the efficacy of promoting democratic change abroad in light of the record of the past three decades."[13]

Their examples are telling: "After we have already seen dictatorships toppled by democratic forces in such seemingly unlikely places as the Philippines, Indonesia, Chile, Nicaragua," why stop now? They do not mention that in both Indonesia and Chile the CIA toppled democratic governments, after which the United States supported two of the most brutal military dictatorships of the twentieth century; that in Nicaragua the allegedly democratizing forces we equipped and called "freedom fighters" fit our own definition of terrorists; or that the "democracy" in the Philippines is purely formal, being controlled by a tiny plutocracy.[14]

On the basis of such grotesque misreadings of history, the hard-nosed secular theorists of the Bush regime, such as Paul Wolfowitz and Richard Perle as well as Kaplan and Kristol, espouse *idealism*. They unapologetically proclaim the "American Idea" as *Pax Americana.* But by defending our unilateralism as not only benevolent but messianic, their Aristotelian-Straussian idealism colludes with the populism of the Christian right, including the president's own evangelical posture, marked by White House prayer meetings. This mixture, which worked for Ronald Reagan, was reintroduced at a new pitch.

This potent merger of elitist idealism with conservative Christian populism has provided the overarching legitimation for our empire. It is specifically in the code of *evil*, furthermore, that this idealism fuses with apocalypticism. Thus the phrase "axis of evil" cunningly conflates the "evil empire" denounced by Reagan with "the axis" powers of World War II. The Bush Doctrine, write Kristol and Kaplan, "signals a return to this earlier era, when Munich, not Vietnam, was the cautionary example."[15] They argue, against Niebuhr, that our temptation is isolationism, not imperialism.

But this attempt to restore "the Great Generation" deploys a fundamental-ist demonization of the Other not needed in WWII or even the Cold War. Defending Bush from his detractors' "howls of derision" over his use of the term "evil," Kaplan and Kristol insist that "as the events of 9/11 remind us, evil exists in this world, and it has consequences." Who can disagree? But with a great logical somersault, they continue: "Fortunately, evil can be defeated. Just as Ronald Reagan's assault on the 'evil empire' was key to top-pling Soviet communism."[16]

This is cryptotheology. Never mind that *biblically* speaking, evil is *never* sim-ply defeated, at least not in history by humans. Evil is often constrained, tricked, or exorcised. Jesus had, for instance, called the "pigs" who were suffering from demon possession "legion," thereby satirizing the police power of the Roman legions. Evil as such is defeated in the Bible, if at all, by the final advent of the Messiah. As Niebuhr argued, America's messianic idealism sabotages the devel-opment of the political wisdom to know that "powerful forces may be beguiled, deflected, and transmuted but never simply annulled or defied."[17]

Whether or not our policies protect us from evil, they certainly depend par-asitically upon its foreign manifestations: without melodramatic figures of evil such as Osama bin Laden and Saddam Hussein, the Bush administration would have continued to founder. As British novelist and commentator Tariq Ali observed, "The leaders of the United States wish to be judged by their choice of enemies rather than the actual state of the world."[18]

Is this halo of morality with which we go forth to "overcome evil" a merely expedient, hypocritical justification—a front for hypercapitalism? My argu-ment is that it is always a mistake to underestimate the sincerity behind this halo. No matter how much and how profitable the U.S. government's falsehoods, it perpetrates them in the name of what it considers a Larger Truth. From the gov-ernment's perspective, the halo holds in place "our American creed" and the "Bush Doctrine"—the defining feature of which is preventive-preemption war. The halo holds together our might with our self-perceived goodness.

But what energizes the halo? What legitimating symbolism, what code of creation, provides the energy, if not that of a deity who is at once all-good and all-mighty? So here is the question for theology: Might it be the very doctrine of divine omnipotence that charges the halo with its holy electricity?

Omnipotence and Preemption

What would omnipotence, a dignified doctrine of classical Christianity and of orthodox Judaism and Islam as well, have to do with any doctrine of imperial human power? If human superpower apes divine power, it is committing the crassest idolatry. If a logic of preventive-preemption is gaining legitimacy from a prior logic of omnipotence—or if the U.S. halo is sucking energy from a theological assumption—religious leaders had better take note. To test for this idolatrous displacement, I would like to host a strange conversation between the Bush-Doctrine idealists and the great idol-smasher John Calvin.

As David Griffin has demonstrated, it is Calvin who most forcefully spells out the implications of traditional theism.[19] Calvin confronts head-on the difficult logic of a power that controls all things. He rejects the easy out—common in his day as well as our own—to say that the omnipotent God only *permits*, rather than actually *causes*, evil things to happen. "God does not permit," Calvin thunders, "but governs by his power." Continuing, he says that "they babble and talk absurdly who, in place of God's Providence, substitute bare permission—as if God sat in a watchtower awaiting chance events, and his judgment thus depended upon human will."[20] Calvin's God, being omnipotent, does not wait for things to happen and then respond.

Do we hear an echo of this doctrine of providence in the doctrine of preventive-preemption? Our National Security Strategy document states: "Given the goals of rogue states and terrorists, the United States can no longer rely on a reactive posture as we have in the past."[21] Preemption, like predestination, is proaction, indeed preaction, not reaction.

That the traditional doctrine of omnipotence makes God responsible for evil as well as good is not a problem for Calvin. What bothers him instead is that "today so many venomous dogs assail this doctrine." Rather familiarly, what matters is to silence the critics, not to examine the merits of their critique. "Paul does not, as do those I have spoken of, labor anxiously to make *false excuses in God's defense*: he only warns that it is unlawful for the clay to quarrel with its potter" (emphasis added).[22] Similarly, the new imperialists eschew argument. They simply say, "A humane future, then, will require an American foreign policy that is *unapologetic, idealistic, assertive and well funded*. America must not only be the world's policeman or its sheriff, it must be its beacon and guide."[23]

"The alternative to American leadership," write Kaplan and Kristol, "is a chaotic, Hobbesian world where there is no authority to thwart aggression, ensure peace and security or enforce international norms." In other words, the horrific chaos that our foreign policy has produced is—if you squint patriotically—really order; our dominance creates freedom; our wars ensure peace; and open defiance of half a century of international law enforces "international norms."

Incomprehensible doublespeak? But omnipotence is precisely the doctrine of God's "incomprehensible providence." Calvin manfully acknowledges the horror of double predestination, including the damnation of unbaptized infants—who were damned only "because it so pleased God." Showing a spark of humanity, Calvin continues: "The decree is dreadful indeed, I confess." But, rather than questioning whether such a dreadful decree could have originated with an all-good deity, he simply suggests that we must "tremble at so deep a mystery."[24] The unquestionable assumption is that nothing happens unless God specifically wills it, no matter how horrific. Sometimes God must shock and awe.

What are we to make of this? God's loving goodness and God's omnipotence might seem, in every event of unjust suffering, to contradict each other. However, by definition, we are told, God's power and love are one. Of course, this traditional unity of attributes becomes a "mystery"—a euphemism for a contradiction—only if the divine power is, with Calvin, understood to be all-controlling. He recognizes the ethical consequences: "when we are *unjustly* wounded by men," Calvin advises, "let us overlook their wickedness (which would but worsen our pain and sharpen our minds to revenge)." Is this a pastoral counsel to love the enemy? Not quite. We are to "learn to believe for certain that whatever our enemy has *wickedly* committed against us was permitted and sent by God's *just* dispensation."[25] In other words: wickedness is just. Of course, few Calvinists—beyond Jerry Falwell—used this logic to legitimate the attack on the Twin Towers.

Yet the logic-defying logic of omnipotence twinned with goodness ultimately sanctions *every* injustice as the will of God. This is a Christianity distant from the prophetic stance of the three Abrahamic traditions, in which God opposes injustice. In these prophetic traditions, it is up to the faithful neither to justify the injustice as God's will nor to seek revenge, but to *enact* God's justice. Historically, of course, there remains plenty of room for ambiguity—both in biblical models, as in the annihilation of the citizens of Jericho, and in present circumstances, where violence must sometimes be risked. Ideally we prevent the buildup of vengefulness that sooner or later irrupts in a terrorist attack. Less ideally, a preemptive strike can be justified before the world in the case of a threat that is genuine and imminent rather than fabricated.

But the Bush doctrine of preventive preemption has sought legitimacy not in terms of defense (mere reaction) but as the promotion of America's "interest in a benevolent international order." America's secular theologians of empire portray this empire as, like God, omnipresent in its benevolence. Kaplan and Kristol say, "American preeminence cannot be maintained from a distance. The US should instead conceive of itself as at once a European power, an Asian power and of course, a Middle Eastern power. It would act as if threats to the interests of our allies are threats to us, which indeed they are."[26] So it is not simply that America will project power unilaterally anywhere it wants. It will also, like God, be already everywhere. As with Calvin, so with the United States. This omnipresence means not just involvement, but dominance.

The American myth of providential exceptionalism, however, remains complex. From our national foundations it inspires not only imperial but also both revolutionary and democratizing codes. And arguably it was deeply wounded by the 9/11 attack. So I have not argued that the doctrine of omnipotence "caused" the doctrine of preventive preemption. Legitimation is not about causal explanation. Rather, the relation resembles what complexity theory calls a "resonance," in which positive feedback rapidly amplifies a coded pattern. This feedback loop, or halo, has been developing for millennia. But its current American code is unprecedented, not only in its sense of sanctity but also in its apocalyptic weaponry and its global reach. Therefore, theological complacency—however much supplemented by progressive activism— will leave untouched the legitimacy of its project.

Despite my deployment of Calvin as an example of a deleterious concept of power, I hasten to add, Calvin is no less important in the *delegitimation* of the U.S. domination project. In Calvin's theology, any construction of any group— any nation, any race, any religion—as unambiguously good, sin-free agents of divine vengeance counts only as crassest idolatry. How then could Reformed Protestantism play such a key role in the development of U.S. culture, not only in the creative and progressive evolution of its communal disciplines, but also in the spirit of capitalism and the worship of human power? A discerning theopolitics reads its guiding texts with constructive ambivalence.

Niebuhr, for instance, took the bull of his own Calvinism by the horns. He embraced the Calvinism that affirms "the grace of divine power, working without immediate regard for the virtues or defects of its recipients (as illustrated by the sun shining 'upon the evil and the good and the rain descending upon the just and the unjust')."[27] But he showed how "any grateful acceptance of God's uncovenanted mercies is easily corrupted from gratitude to self-congratulation" when it "represents particular divine acts directly correlated to particular human and historical situations"—when, in other words, this acceptance of divine mercy yields to the logic of omnipotence.

Niebuhr showed the roots of the American Protestant identification of *affluence* with *blessing* in Calvin himself, who declared that "there is no question that riches should be in the portion of the godly rather than the wicked, for godliness hath the promise in this life as well as the life to come."[28] In the formative period of the Union, American prosperity seems to have widely supported the notion of our special favor: "If any people have been lifted up to advantages and privileges, we are the people." So said William Stoughton

(1631–1701), who continued, "We have had the eye and hand of God working everywhere for our good."[29] But it is precisely here that the acute sense of sin is sabotaged by a notion of preemptive providence, which fosters our world-threatening innocence.

One paragraph in Niebuhr's chapter titled "The American Future" made my hair stand on end. Writing more than a half-century ago, he warned that our technocratic notion that history can be mastered like nature

> could tempt us to lose patience with the tortuous course of history. We might be driven to hysteria by its inevitable frustrations. We might be tempted to bring the whole of modern history to a tragic conclusion by one final and mighty effort to overcome its frustrations. The political term for such an effort is "preventive war." It is not an immediate temptation; but it could become so in the next decade or two. A democracy can not, of course, engage in an explicit preventive war.[30]

But we *have*: explicitly, doctrinally, and without imminent or even long-term threat to ourselves. In the aftermath of this decision for preventive-preemptive attacks, the democratic experiment hangs in the balance.

After Omnipotence

A theology of omnipotence electrifies the halo of American domination. Where then does the idolatry lie? In the fact that the United States plays God? Or, as I would put it, in the fact that it imitates a *false* God? Does the idolatry lie in our emulation of a divine superpower? Or in our confusion of God with omnipotence in the first place? A theopolitics of omnipotence is clearly at work in American imperialism. But is there already an imperialism within the doctrine of omnipotence?

In discussing the conversion of the Roman Empire to Christianity, Alfred North Whitehead—neither simply an idealist nor a realist, but both—wrote of "the deeper idolatry, of the fashioning of God in the image of the Egyptian, Persian, and Roman imperial rulers." Pointing out one effect of this idolatry, he said that the resulting doctrine of "a transcendent creator, at whose fiat the world came into being, and whose imposed will it obeys, is the fallacy which has infused tragedy into the histories of Christianity and of [Islam]." Then comes one of the great propositions of Christian autocritique: "The church gave unto God the attributes that belonged exclusively to Caesar."[31]

There you have pretty much the origin of what is called process theology, whose leading exponents still fan the flames of what Whitehead called the flickering Galilean humility. Process theology's God, who works by "lure" rather than domination, cannot legitimate projects of dominance. Griffin has called this a shift from the power of coercion to the power of persuasion—the democratic art par excellence.[32]

Some critics think of this as a doctrine of impotence. But impotence is not the only alternative to Calvinistic omnipotence. Another alternative discerns at the heart of the universe a wisdom of open ends, a strange attractor amid indeterminacy and its complex determinations. Calvin is right: God is not sitting in a watchtower, impassively awaiting the results. God is there, in the midst of every event. But Calvin assumed that for God to *participate* in an event is for God to *control* it. To be sure, God remembers every sparrow, numbers every hair. But does this mean—as Calvin in defending double predestination says—that God *determines* which of my hairs will turn gray today? Or might we affirm with Calvin that "God" names a dark incomprehensibility, not to be reduced to the anthropomorphic terms of human love or justice. Thus Job's bewildering whirlwind. But then why reduce the mystery to an all-too-human, all-too-masculine, and all-too-imperial idol of power? Why turn a humbling mystery into a mystification of injustice?

Many Christians are ready for such a transcoding of cosmic power. This transcoding also has resonance for many Jews, Muslims, Hindus, Buddhists, ethical agnostics, and others. For there is an ocean of *satyagraha*, of truth-force, waiting to surge into this new millennium. Faith seems everywhere—in spite of the various fundamentalisms—on the verge of coming of age. It is in part blocked by liberal incredulity—even many thoughtful people assume that faith requires some big guy in the sky. They are repelled by the theopolitics of power. They can see only, on the one hand, *a manic will to power called omnipotence* and, on the other hand, a *depressive sentimentality called love*. For the classical fusion of goodness with omnipotence creates in fact not unity but a bipolar disorder.

To heal the religious schizophrenia of love and power, power itself first needs recoding. Then another kind of love, a divinely *infinite desire*, might make itself felt—a love that is the opposite, as the Jewish philosopher Emmanuel Levinas suggests, of an *imperial totality*. Such a love desires our fullest becoming—our *genesis*—as individuals, as peoples, as religions, as nations, as creatures inextricably embedded within the interdependencies of the creation. It therefore lets responsibility for the well-being of the earth fall squarely back on the shoulders of us earthlings. As the matrix of spiritual codes is enriched by process, liberation, feminist, and ecological theologians,[33] these theologians support a range of movements that Richard Falk identifies with "globalization from below."[34] They do not reject the politics of theology or the theology of politics, but move desirously toward a theopolitics of becoming.

The Spirit of this wider, wilder, achingly beautiful creation does sometimes seem to be revealing itself. Not making itself known—we only *know* our own metaphors. So let us make them as rich in justice and "the care that nothing be lost," as poetically alive and even scripturally resonant, as possible. Let the hierarchical universe of unilateral and omnipotent sovereignty fade into a more wildly democratic cosmos of unpredictable and uncontrollable—but never unordered—interrelations. God is called upon not as a unilateral superpower but as a relational force, not an omnipotent creator from nothing, imposing order upon inert entities, but the lure to a self-organizing complexity, creating out of the chaos—the *tohu-vabohu* of which Genesis 1 speaks.

Recall that for Hannah Arendt, legitimacy entails narratives of creation, indeed, birth narratives. How would such a shift—to a narrative of beginnings that is more faithful both biblically and materially—alter the originative codes of legitimation? Might the world begin to appear neither as the work of pre-emptive transcendence, nor of random chance, but of the unpredictable, uncontrollable, and uncontrolling wisdom of the whirlwind?

This theology does not apologize for uncertainty. Faith is not a matter of certainty but of courage.[35] Faith takes the primordial American value of liberty to heart: Nothing important can be imposed by coercion. Freedom will not be achieved by dominance, legitimacy by lies, law by unilateralism, peace by war, Christian love by hatred of the Other. That coercive, imperialistic piety needs to be, and can be, replaced by a democratizing spirituality.

The American democratic idea has always been flawed by its imprint of empire, class, race, and gender-and-sexual injustice. So has Christian love. Might we augment both? Can we broadcast to our people this self-evident truth—that human democracy, like the love of God, will not legitimate any project of global dominance? Democracy will either extend to our international relations or it will die at home—before we ever quite gave it birth.[36]

Chapter 8

Commonwealth and Empire

John B. Cobb Jr.

The New Empire

Empires have dominated the Western world for thousands of years. There was a period in Mesopotamia when cities did not require walls. Presumably they were well supported by the agricultural lands that surrounded them and did not need what they did not have. However, as population grew, soils became salty so that harvests declined, and maintaining irrigation ditches became more difficult, the city-states ceased to be self-sufficient and found it profitable to conquer one another. From that time to this, empire has been the rule, not the exception, in the civilized world.

The ideology of empire is fairly simple. It expresses the desires to add to one's wealth and to dominate over others, desires that seem to be found among at least some segments of all "civilized" societies. The ideology assumes that if one group is able to assert its will over others, then it is superior to them and has the right to exploit them. Typically, the imperial power extends its control as far as it can. The actual superiority is military, but the military success is typically accompanied by claims of cultural and moral superiority and, in modernity, of racial superiority as well.

The United States is built on imperial expansion across the continent. This expansion exterminated most of the inhabitants and displaced most of the rest. It subjugated all who survived. It was justified by claims of cultural, religious, and racial superiority. Long before the conquest of what is now the continental United States was complete, the nation declared its hegemony over most of the rest of the Western Hemisphere. As European empires declined after World War II, the United States extended its dominance elsewhere. It organized much of the world over against the Soviet empire. When the Soviet Union collapsed, the United States extended its hegemonic claims globally.

Opposition to the American Empire

Although some people proclaim the day of American global empire with enthu-siasm, there are, of course, counterideals and countermovements, as there have been throughout history. Most subjects of foreign empires resent them and resist them when they can. Over time, empires have all collapsed. Often they simply gave way to other empires. Sometimes there have been periods in which in large areas no one nation has been militarily strong enough to con-quer others. Within Europe, for example, policies aimed at maintaining a bal-ance of power worked rather well for a time.

In addition, some persons—the authors of this book among them—have opposed empire and imperial ambition in principle. We believe that there are other ways to order life and the relations among the peoples of the world, and we favor those ways. We share these convictions with millions of others.

Indeed, during much of my lifetime, "imperialism" has been a word with strongly negative connotations, at least in the United States. We told ourselves our own national story in such a way as to obscure, or altogether conceal, its imperialistic character. We were morally pleased by the liberation of Euro-pean colonies after World War II, and we did not acknowledge to ourselves our complicity, and leadership, in establishing, through economic policies, a neocolonial global system, ordered largely to our benefit. Most Americans still resist a realistic picture of our imperialistic history. Even those who advo-cated empire generally avoided use of the term, at least until quite recently.

The call in the 1990s by the Project for the New American Century for a *Pax Americana*, modeled on Roman and British imperialism, brought the real-ity of American empire to the fore.[1] It has helped to bring the long-term impe-rialism of the United States into clearer view. It is now possible to have conferences about it. Those of us who oppose imperialism in principle hope to appeal to the lingering negative connotations of the term, to arouse more Americans to work against the extension and intensification of the imperial-ist thrust of our past. We even hope that there may be some repentance for our past acts and a turning in different directions.

Most people have difficulty imagining a world very different from the one in which they live. We have lived for thousands of years in a world in which those who are able to do so have exploited others. When this nearly universal tendency leads to the extension of power over a considerable area, we typi-cally recognize this as empire. In short, all the civilized world—meaning the world that came into existence with the rise of cities—has known for thou-sands of years is a world in which the real question was not whether there would be empires, but who would succeed in establishing them.

"Realists," therefore, concentrate on making sure that theirs is the successful imperial nation. If that is not possible, then they seek to position their nation as favorably as possible in relation to the imperial power. If leaders of successful nations are humane in their attitudes, they may be interested in moderating the suffering of subject people and even in improving the lot of some of the ruled. Those lacking any real concern for the well-being of their subjects may still recognize that, in order to maintain empire, it is well to give some benefits, real or apparent, to the ruled.

In this book, however, we are not asking how to make American hegemony more humane or more beneficial to the world. We oppose empire as such.

The Source of Contra-Empire Ideals

My first question is, then, where have the values and ideals that oppose empire arisen? Where have we learned values that differ so dramatically from those that actually govern the behavior of nations? The answer is, of course, complex. These values have arisen in many places, as thoughtful people have sought to imagine a better world than the one that is controlled by military and economic power.

However, some historical generalizations are useful. Chiefly, these contra-imperial ideals can be traced to what Karl Jaspers has taught us to call the Axial Age, the period during the middle of the first millennium before the Common Era, when the philosophies and religious traditions that still shape much of the mind of the world came into existence. They arose in an imperial period that evoked individual reflection as a response.[2]

This reflection was about how the world and human society are actually to be constructed and about what is truly valuable and worthwhile for individual people in their relations with others. The answers arose not so much from the study of ancient texts as from fresh thought and insight. They were diverse. The answers of Confucius and Laotzu differed from one another and from those of Plato and Aristotle and the Stoics. All of these answers differed from those of the sages of India and Persia. And the answers of the Hebrew prophets were different still. Some answers dealt more directly than others with an alternative to the mind-set that caused and brought about imperialism. But all the answers proposed values that, if taken with full seriousness, would lead away from imperialism.

The great figures of the Axial Age are widely admired. They all have had some serious followers, and many other people who are little affected by their actual teachings have paid lip service to them. Even serious followers have, for the most part, compromised between their teachings and what seems to be required to survive and prosper in the real world. Nevertheless, to this day, most of the idealism that leads to opposition to imperialism finds its source in the ideals generated in this period.

I am not trying in this chapter to provide a balanced account of the contributions of the several great traditions. Instead, I am focusing on the West, where the main sources of values and ideals are Greek and Hebrew. I am also judging, without argument, that the deeper source of our contra-imperial ideals is Hebrew. These values have been mediated to us primarily through two figures who lived after the Axial Age, but who stood in the tradition of the Hebrew prophets: Jesus and Muhammad. In Europe and North America, thus far, Jesus has played the larger role.

The Anti-Imperialistic Ideals of Jesus

For much of Western history, the great majority of the population affirmed the authority of Jesus. Today, commitment to Christianity has declined in leadership circles, but the influence of Jesus extends far beyond the circle of those of us who identify ourselves as Christians. Indeed, sometimes the influence seems more effective when it is not so strongly mediated by the institutional church. And, of course, Jesus, like all classical figures, is widely influential even among those who do not know the sources of their values.

Sadly, the anti-imperial elements of Jesus' message have not dominated the doctrines proclaimed by the church through much of its history. These elements were taken with some seriousness in the early church, where many Christians refused military service. The early church definitely taught people to seek goals other than wealth and power and to withdraw their admiration or envy from those who were successful by those worldly standards. It produced within the Roman world a society in which the social ranking of the larger society was not determinative.

I do not mean to idealize the early church. But it would also be a mistake to ignore or deny its resistance to the ideology that supported empire. The imperial rulers were not foolish to persecute it.

When, finally, the empire decided to ally itself with the church instead of persecuting it, the church changed more than the empire. From then on, even if it continued teachings that were in principle contra-imperial, its practice was to support the emperor and follow his lead on many matters. To this day, the dominant theory and practice of the mainline churches are markedly compromised by the change in their relation to actual power. It would be unfair to say that their contra-imperial teachings have had no effect on the exercise of power by imperial rulers, but it would be hard to argue that Christian emperors have been profoundly different from other imperial rulers in their major policies and actions.

Some parts of church life remained relatively free from this involvement with political power, and there the influence of Jesus' message could be found. The Christian ideal of a life lived for values other than power and wealth shaped the monastic tradition. Of course, this too was often corrupted, but the ideal remained powerful. As long as the West regarded itself as Christendom, its greatest heroes were mostly poor and politically and militarily powerless. They denied themselves possessions and the exercise of force, and even children, so as to give themselves more wholly to the service of God and humanity. Aiming at the acquisition of wealth was not admired.

Only in the Renaissance were the contra-imperial ideals of Christianity directly challenged. Machiavelli in the sixteenth century began this process with respect to political power, but it was not until the eighteenth century, the height of the Western Enlightenment, that the quest for personal gain was morally celebrated and success in this quest once again admired. The retreat of Christian values before the ideal of increasing total wealth through self-interested efforts accelerated in the second half of the twentieth century.

In the Middle Ages, the contra-imperial ideal expressed itself more fully in protests against the actual behavior of the church than in that behavior itself. Such protests appeared throughout the Middle Ages and were usually ruthlessly suppressed. Francis of Assisi's protests were the most successful. He was too popular for the church to attack him directly, but those who followed him most closely among later generations of Franciscans were not so fortunate.

Radical ideas derived from Jesus reappeared in the left wing of the Reformation. Their advocates were persecuted by both Catholics and Protestants. But some groups survived. The Quakers to this day take the message of Jesus with unusual seriousness. They are best known for their rejection of social hierarchy and of war, and for their emphasis on nonviolent resistance of evil.

Mahatma Gandhi was influenced by Jesus' Sermon on the Mount in his development of nonviolent resistance to British rule in India. Martin Luther King Jr. also sought to follow Jesus and learned much from Gandhi about how to do this. Many others have been influenced both directly by Jesus and indirectly through Gandhi and King. Jesus' influence in shaping a contra-imperial understanding and practice is still very much alive.

The *Basileia Theou*

Today, the clearest and most accurate way of presenting Jesus' contra-imperial vision is by focusing on his teaching about what he called the *basileia theou*. This Greek phrase has usually been translated into English as "the kingdom of God." The author of the Gospel of Matthew preferred not to speak so directly of God and so wrote more often of "the kingdom of heaven."

Although these terms have not been prominent through most of church history in relation to the teaching of Jesus, there has now, for some time, been wide agreement among scholars that Jesus' message centers on his proclamation of the *basileia theou*. To bring together the contra-imperial teaching of Jesus under this heading may help to make clearer its subversive meaning and to unleash its power in a time of special need.

Jesus' teaching is not only contra-imperial. It is also contra–religious-establishment. Christians have liked to suppose that this dimension of Jesus' teaching opposed only the Jewish establishment of his time. But the frequent suppression of Jesus' teaching by the Christian establishment, along with the fact that this teaching reappeared chiefly in movements protesting that establishment, reminds us that Jesus' critique is far more radical.

All three of the Synoptic Gospels—Matthew, Mark, and Luke—locate the proclamation of the *basileia theou* at or near the outset of Jesus' public ministry. In Luke's account, when the crowds tried to keep Jesus in Capernaum to continue his healing ministry there, he said, "I must proclaim the good news of the *basileia theou* to the other cities also; for I was sent for this purpose" (4:43). Mark writes: "Now after John was arrested, Jesus came to Galilee, proclaiming the good news of God, and saying, 'The time is fulfilled and the *basileia theou* is come near; repent and believe in the good news'" (1:14–15). Matthew states that after Jesus settled in Capernaum, he "began to proclaim, 'Repent, for the kingdom of heaven has come near'" (4:17).

The implication in the words attributed to Jesus in these passages is that his entire message consists of an unpacking of this proclamation. This conclusion fits with the accounts that follow. Many of the parables and other sayings are explicitly about the *basileia theou*, and even those parables where the term does not occur can well be interpreted as dealing with this topic. The same is true of the Beatitudes. The *basileia theou* also plays the pivotal role in the prayer Jesus taught his disciples to pray. His emphasis on a *basileia* that was not Roman played a major role in the decision to crucify him. All three Synoptic Gospels report that an inscription over his head on the cross indicated that he was condemned for claiming to be "king of the Jews."

The centrality of the *basileia theou* in the ministry of Jesus requires no scholarship to discover. It is apparent to any casual reader of the Synoptic Gospels. But the church has made little of it over the centuries. One reason has been that the majority of Christians over the millennia have not been focused on Jesus' message as depicted in the Synoptic Gospels. For very many, Christianity became a religion of personal salvation, emphasizing salvation from sin and guilt and, of course, hell. This emphasis was derived from a certain interpretation of the letters of Paul and the Gospel of John—an interpretation that required a good deal of creativity on the part of the church. In addition, the church liked to apply to *itself* much of what Jesus said about the *basileia theou*. Many Christians with less institutional interest interpreted the *basileia theou* as otherworldly, not as a condition to be realized in this world.

In this context, the Synoptic Gospels were read more to marvel at Jesus' miracles than to listen to his message. Actually, the Gospels report that this was a problem for Jesus himself: People were more interested in being healed of their physical sicknesses than in hearing his teachings. For these and other reasons, the *basileia theou*, as described by Jesus, played very little role in Christian history until rather recently. Such influence as Jesus' message did have was largely independent of this teaching.

By the latter part of the nineteenth century, however, the centrality of the *basileia theou* was widely acknowledged in progressive circles. In the United States, preachers stirred by the suffering of factory workers in the newly industrial cities developed what came to be called the Social Gospel. The leaders of the Social Gospel movement understood themselves to be recovering the message of Jesus himself, which, they believed, was primarily about a new social reality rather than how individuals could attain an otherworldly salvation.

Since World War I, regrettably, theoretical and practical problems have led theology in other directions. The *basileia theou*, so central to Jesus, has again faded from the vocabulary of preaching and teaching in the churches of the United States. But when we confront the ideology of empire, it is past time to revive and renew it.

The Commonwealth of God

I have been using the Greek phrase, *basileia theou*, because I do not want the connotations of the various English translations to cloud our understanding before we have considered what Jesus himself intended. We have gotten accustomed to talking about *agape*, because "love" means so many different things that it does not communicate the New Testament message well. For a while, we talked a lot about *koinonia* in order to capture the rich meaning of the original term, which is too easily lost in such English translations as "church," "assembly," "congregation," and even "fellowship." So perhaps we should try to highlight the New Testament meaning of *basileia theou* by using, initially, the Greek phrase.

The standard translation, the "kingdom of God," is not wrong, but it can be misleading. Kingdom implies a masculine ruler, whereas the Greek does not. A quite common translation today is the "reign of God." That phrase avoids the gender issue, but it accents the controlling action of God. A better translation would be the "realm of God," which mixes connotations of God's rule with that of a sphere, not necessarily geographical, in which God rules.

The Jesus Seminar has settled on "empire of God." This translation has the advantage of leading quite directly to contrasting it with the Roman and American empires. But it only heightens the hierarchical and authoritarian connotations, which are conspicuous by their absence in Jesus' account.

Jesus' description does not emphasize God's rule. The closest Jesus comes to a definition of the *basileia theou* is in the Lord's Prayer, where the second line of the couplet explains the meaning of the first. "Your *basileia* come" means the same as "Your will be done, on earth as it is in heaven." Now this could, perhaps, be taken to mean that God rules in an authoritarian and controlling manner in heaven, and we are asking that God extend this rule to earth. But the prayer is not directed to our king or emperor or the almighty one. It is addressed to "our Father." Matthew 6 gives us only the Greek for father, but elsewhere (Mark 14:36) we learn how Jesus addressed God in his own language, Aramaic. He prayed to "Abba," which is equivalent to "Papa" or "Daddy," certainly not to king or emperor. Jesus' teaching about God emphasizes God's *agape* and compassion, not God's sovereign control. To ask that God's will be done on earth as in heaven is certainly to ask for a transformation of the earth, but it is not asking for God to take control and impose an arbitrary rule on the earth.

The best English translation may be "commonwealth." This term, besides not emphasizing the controlling power of a ruler, suggests that the realm may be organized for the common good. Hence, the title of this chapter. I am not proposing this as *the* correct translation or as one that is free from problematic connotations, but it may be relatively open to being filled with the meanings Jesus had in mind.

So how did Jesus understand the commonwealth of God? He understood it to be a world in which God's will is done, God's purposes are fulfilled. Jesus saw his own work and the community that developed around him as foreshadowing that sort of world. It was characterized by the healing of the sick, the release of prisoners, and freeing people from guilt. The thirsty receive water, the hungry are fed, and the naked are clothed. To come into the fellowship that foreshadows the commonwealth of God, the rich must share their wealth. Within that fellowship, the boundaries that separate people are erased. Sinners—that is, people who do not fulfill the law——eat with those who do. Loving relations supersede obedience to law as the character of the commonwealth.

During its heyday, the Social Gospel rightly emphasized that in a society in which ordinary Christians have some capacity to shape the policies of their governments and the character of their local communities, the implications of Jesus' message extend to political action. In addition to more direct efforts to heal the sick, feed the hungry, and break down barriers between people, Christians should envisage better social structures and seek to enact legislation that can improve the situation for far more people than does direct action. Jesus' teaching about the commonwealth thus became the basis for intimately connecting the life of the Christian with social action directed especially to the improvement of the lot of the poor. The New Deal grew in part out of the Social Gospel.

The Social Gospel flourished in the first two decades of the twentieth century, but the First World War hurt it, and it barely survived the Second World War. The events of the twentieth century undercut it for several reasons.

First, it was connected with an exaggerated optimism. The still-important magazine *The Christian Century* received its name from the confidence of Social Gospel leaders that, in the twentieth century, Christianity would bring the commonwealth of God to the whole world. This process would involve democracy, modern science, technology, medical care, universal education, and the abolition of war and poverty. When supposedly Christian nations, instead, led the planet into the horror of two world wars and the Jewish Holocaust, this kind of expectation seemed very unrealistic indeed.

The optimism and the sharp disillusionment that followed these horrors were connected with a separation of the content of the commonwealth of God from Jesus' emphasis that it is a work of God, rather than something to be achieved by independent human effort. When I grew up, in the late days of the Social Gospel, we spoke of "building the kingdom." Events taught us that we are quite incapable of doing so and that part of the problem is our own sinfulness.

Second, biblical scholars raised many questions about the way the Social Gospel preachers had interpreted Jesus' understanding of the commonwealth. Some argued that for Jesus the coming of the commonwealth of God could only be an apocalyptic event that would come through a supernatural act of God in the last days. If so, the whole idea of seeing our social action as related to Jesus' message was undercut. Rudolf Bultmann, the greatest New Testament scholar of the post–World War II generation, interpreted Jesus' message in individualistic, existentialist terms, so that the social dimension seemed to be a misunderstanding.[3] Others suggested that the commonwealth of God is the reality actually brought into being by Jesus and continued in the community of believers. This interpretation could emphasize the importance of congregational life, but the nerve of social action was cut.

It is time to recognize that the Social Gospel writers were closer to the truth than these alternatives. They were profoundly wrong to whatever extent they failed to recognize the depths of human sinfulness and its capacity to derail movements toward a world in which God's purposes are realized. They were profoundly wrong to whatever extent they regarded Christian action as separable from the working of God's grace in creatures. But they were not wrong in believing that one who takes Jesus' message seriously is called in our day to work for the improvement of the lot of the poor through political channels as well as private and ecclesiastical ones. Today that means that we are called to work against American empire.

The closest equivalent of the Social Gospel that has flourished in more recent years is Liberation Theology. It also appeals to Jesus' teaching about the commonwealth of God. It provides in many ways an extension and deepening of the Social Gospel as well as a correction. Too often the Social Gospel was only a call on the rich and powerful to use their wealth and power more justly. Liberation Theology, in contrast, aims to empower the poor and oppressed. It is more revolutionary than reformist.

The Social Gospel, being closely connected to the struggle for justice for industrial workers, who were mostly recent immigrants from Europe, had far too little to say about justice for non-European ethnic groups. It did not prepare us for our current understanding of how Euro-Americans have oppressed and exploited African Americans and Native Americans, for example. Paying attention to Jesus' message should have brought these matters into the center of attention. It certainly must today.

The Social Gospel teachings about the place of women were generally positive, but they sound outdated today. There was no deep recognition of the evils of patriarchy. The overcoming of patriarchy in the commonwealth of God must today be central to any renewal of this theme.

There is much more to be said of the limitations of the Social Gospel and even of the Liberation Theologies that have renewed the theme of the commonwealth of God. The ecological dimension, for example, has had difficulty being fully expressed through these movements, whereas it may well be the locus of the most important danger of all. Also, both movements have been clearer in their economic teachings than in their analysis of national military power. The threat of U.S. imperial rule over the whole world must certainly be addressed more directly in faithfulness to Jesus.

Although the social gospel writers clearly understood that Jesus taught us to measure our actions by their effects on the poor, they did not fully appreciate the reversal of values proclaimed by Jesus. In this respect, too, the Liberation Theologies do better. Consider who, according to Jesus, is truly blessed or happy. In Luke, it is the poor, the hungry, those who weep, and those who are hated and excluded and defamed (6:20–22).

Luke follows the beatitudes with a series of "woes." They are equally telling. "Woe to you who are rich, for you have received your consolation. Woe to you who are full now, for you will be hungry. Woe to you who are laughing now, for you will mourn and weep. Woe to you when all speak well of you, for that is what their ancestors did to the false prophets" (6:24–26). Much the same point is made by Jesus' parable of Lazarus and the rich man (Luke 16:19–31). Matthew tones down this point in his version of the Sermon on the Mount by speaking of the "poor in spirit" instead of simply the "poor." For this reason scholars assume that Luke's account is more authentic. But Matthew's report of Jesus' teaching on possessions is extreme enough. "Give to anyone who begs from you, and do not refuse anyone who wants to borrow from you" (5:42). Further, "you cannot serve God and wealth" (6:24).

These passages are far from the only ones that reverse well-established assumptions about what is desirable. Matthew, Mark, and Luke all report that Jesus stated that it is harder for a rich man to enter the commonwealth of God than for a camel to go though the eye of a needle (e.g., Matt. 19:24). Addressing respectable Jews, Jesus said that the despised tax collectors and prostitutes would enter the commonwealth of God before them. When asked who is greatest in the commonwealth, he said that unless adults become like little children, they cannot enter it.

Occasionally the contrast with Roman rule is direct and explicit. "You know that the rulers of the Gentiles lord it over them, and their great ones are tyrants over them. It will not be so among you; but whoever wishes to be great among you must be your servant, and whoever wishes to be first among you must be your slave; just as the Son of Man came not to be served but to serve, and to give his life a ransom for many" (Matt. 20:25–28). The reference to Jesus' death is unlikely to be from Jesus, but John reports a more immediate and practical expression of service on Jesus' part in his story of Jesus washing the feet of the disciples (John 13:1–11).

The Task for Christians Today

Clearly the commonwealth of God is not modeled on the Roman Empire, and no one who wants to implement Jesus' profound reversal of values would try to create an American empire. His message is fertile seed for contra-imperial ideals. The problem arises when one tries to imagine the kind of order a person moved by this reversal of values should seek in the world, or even in the church. A few try hard, with some success, to live quite directly by these values in their personal and communal lives. For most of us, just as with the church throughout the centuries, practical decisions and actions, and even serious envisioning, entail compromise.

This is not a problem just for Christians who try to take Jesus seriously. It is a problem for all those who are revolted by the imperialistic actions of our nation. On the whole, we stand in the prophetic tradition, which is much clearer in its denunciations than it its positive proposals. We know that if we proposed, and then succeeded in bringing into being, different institutions, the same principles that we appeal to against empire would count against these new institutions as well.

All institutions develop hierarchies. The lust for power and greed for wealth do not disappear. Revolutions that seek justice for the poor can end in massive oppression of all.

Recognizing this, one conclusion that we must take very seriously as Christians is that our task is primarily, perhaps exclusively, criticism. Whatever society we encounter, we will measure it in relation to the commonwealth of God and find it wanting. We will pronounce God's judgment upon it.

There is no question as to the importance of this prophetic role. There will always be much to denounce. Without repeated recalling of the normative standards, even the best society will quickly degenerate into corruption. Also, identifying any society too closely with the commonwealth of God makes difficult the task of noting the compromises and distortions that characterize its actual functioning. Such identification weakens the credibility of the gospel for those who suffer from the inevitable abuses of even good societies.

Nevertheless, to limit the Christian role to prophetic criticism is a counsel of despair. I do not want to be part of an imperial power. Furthermore, the quest for imperial power inevitably weakens the freedom that I prize, at the center of power as well as elsewhere. American imperial power is largely in the service of an economic order that disempowers both individuals and whole nations and intensifies inequality everywhere. Both the military and the economic dimensions of the quest for empire hasten the ecological catastrophe that looms nearer and nearer ahead. I do not accept the conclusion that those of us who dread this outcome have no alternative proposals to offer.

My own mentor, Alfred North Whitehead, suggested that whereas we cannot follow Jesus' message straightforwardly in the course of history, it offers a way of evaluating societies.[4] That society in which it becomes more possible to live according to Jesus' values is better. Clearly a society in which people can survive only through cutthroat competition does not measure up well. The same is true of a society that invites its members to take pride in militarily imposing their collective will on others.

Whitehead's proposal can be used quite practically. We can ask: In what kind of society could people live in communities in which service to one another counted for more than wealth or power? In what kind of society could business be profitably conducted without placing profits above people and community? In what kind of society could the many smaller communities aim to support one another, rather than to compete with one another? In what kind of society could people renounce the use of force even in self-defense?

Obviously, we will never achieve perfection with regard to such ideals. But the impossibility of perfection does not mean that improvements are impossible. We can identify times and places in which societies have done much better in these respects than our society now does. Not all societies have been organized, as ours now is, in the service of wealth and global domination. We can learn from other societies that have put human well-being for all ahead of wealth for a few. We can also learn from those people who have studied and implemented cooperative and genuinely democratic processes as well as patterns of nonviolent resistance.

It is important not to expect too much. Even if a society organizes itself so as to make possible small communities in which people place human well-being above profit and power, that will not ensure that all, or even most, such communities will develop in that direction. That will happen only where the values in question are deeply internalized. A healthy society will create a context where healthy community is possible, but it must also be prepared to set some limits to the abuses it will tolerate in its member communities.

Although we cannot move in any direct way from the contra-imperial values we affirm to advocacy of particular governmental structures, policies, and international relations, we should not hesitate to assert some generalities. For example, the poor are more likely to be taken seriously as human beings if they have an effective voice in government. This requires not only their formal enfranchisement, but also educational systems and media that view issues from their perspective, and the reduction of the power of money in government.

In international affairs, we can confidently assert that moving from imperial control to shared power among the nations and to the rule of law is genuine progress, however remote it may be from the direct expression of the contra-imperial values we affirm. Strengthening and democratizing the United Nations is surely better than undermining its authority and weakening its ability to enforce its rules.

Sadly, there has never been a time in American history when so many have so articulately identified the God of Christian faith with an idol. Today "God" is understood by many to sanction American capitalism, consumerism, and empire. Identifying "God" with American interests and policies, they can view all opposition to the United States as the expression of evil. They pay no attention to Jesus' warning against judging others, or even to his vivid criticism of trying to remove a speck from another's eye while having a log firmly lodged in one's own (Matt. 7:1–5). Indeed, they may worship a cosmic ruler who came to earth to save them and sanction their country. They may even give lip service to the historical Jesus, calling him their favorite philosopher, but they ignore his teaching. Jesus said it is not those who say, "Lord, Lord," who will be saved, but those who do the will of the God whom Jesus called "Abba"—a very different God from the American idol (Matt. 7:21).

Despite all this, Jesus' teaching of the commonwealth of God keeps breaking through, sometimes in the church, sometimes elsewhere. For many of us, even some who do not recognize this fact, it is the deepest grounds for opposition to American empire—or any other empire. Despite all the imperialism and lust for wealth that have shaped so much of American history, there is also in that history an influence of the actual message of Jesus. We who call ourselves Christians are called to fan the sparks of that message into a flame that can help to reverse the headlong plunge of our nation into the lust for world domination.

Chapter 9

Resurrection and Empire

David Ray Griffin

Christian faith is, at least arguably, most centrally a resurrection faith, based
on belief in the resurrection of Jesus. In this chapter, I ask what this belief
should imply about the response of American Christians to the realization that
we live in the most extensive empire there has ever been.

A first point to recall is that Jesus lived in an occupied country—a country
occupied by the most extensive empire the world had ever known. By the time
of the birth of Jesus, Rome had subjected most of the known earth to its rule,
and the goal of Augustus Caesar was "to conquer what remained."[1]

Like all empires, the Roman Empire was brutal. Those territories already
subjugated were kept in line by producing "awe and terror" in their peoples.[2]
Rome practiced what we would today call "state terror." Although states today
like to restrict the term *terrorism* to the nonstate variety—the terrorism of the
weak—that variety is always far less deadly than state-sponsored terrorism.

Rome practiced terror not because Romans were sadistic but because terrorism was deemed effective. What Rome cared about most was what it called
"honor." "What mattered most [to the Roman elite]," says Susan Mattern,
"was how the empire [was] perceived by foreigners and subjects. . . . Terror
and vengeance were instruments for maintaining the empire's image."[3]

We can understand this concept of "honor" because it is the same thing the
United States has called "credibility." Long after it became clear that America's war in Vietnam was a disastrous mistake, countless political and military leaders argued year after year that we could not leave, because we would
lose "credibility." And so we continued to lose tens of thousands of American
soldiers, and to kill hundreds of thousands of Vietnamese people, year after
bloody year, all for the sake of maintaining our credibility.[4]

In the same way now—after it has become clear that America's invasion
of Iraq was at best a disastrous mistake, at worst an illegal war of imperial
aggression, with mounting evidence that the intelligence about weapons of

mass destruction was fabricated by the Bush administration—our leaders tell us that we cannot leave, because we would lose credibility.

An empire can maintain its honor or credibility, its leaders invariably hold, only if everyone knows that it will allow no challenge to its hegemony to go unpunished.

Rome would, in fact, respond to every act of disobedience disproportionately, often slaughtering vast numbers of people. By the time of Jesus, the Roman legions had killed tens of thousands of people in Galilee and had enslaved many more. One of the most traumatic attacks was the burning of Sepphoris, which was only a few miles from Nazareth, at about the time of Jesus' birth.[5]

Besides slaughtering and enslaving people, Rome had another terrorist method for deterring future challengers to its rule: crucifixion. Both Cicero and Josephus called it the worst form of death. The victims of this tactic of state terrorism were displayed in prominent places for all to see.[6] As one Roman put it: "Whenever we crucify the condemned, the most crowded roads are chosen, where the most people can see and be moved by this terror. For penalties relate not so much to retribution as to their exemplary effect."[7]

In Vietnam, American leaders talked about the "demonstration effect" of unleashing our destructive power against the country, saying that it would prevent other peoples from challenging U.S. power.[8] William Bundy argued, for example, that even if the bombing of North Vietnam failed, it would be worth doing because it would "set a higher price for the future upon all adventures of guerrilla warfare."[9]

Crucifixion was Rome's way of saying: If you dare to challenge our authority, this is where you will end up. Jesus would have been well aware of this likelihood. Some two thousand rebels had been crucified near the time of his birth.[10]

We need to be clear that Jesus *was* killed by representatives of the Roman Empire. Crucifixions could be authorized only by such representatives. One problem with books and movies that continue to portray the death of Jesus as due primarily to the Jewish authorities is, of course, that they tend to perpetuate anti-Jewish sentiments among Christians. But another problem is that these portrayals perpetuate the idea that Jesus' criticisms were purely religious, rather than being simultaneously political and economic. As Richard Horsley says in his recent book *Jesus and Empire*, the fact that Jesus was crucified is one of many factors showing that he was preaching an "anti-imperial gospel."[11] "That Jesus was *crucified* by the Roman governor," says Horsley, "stands as a vivid symbol of his historical relationship with the Roman imperial order."[12]

Given this understanding, what would the resurrection of Jesus have meant? It was, of course, taken to mean many things. But one thing that it clearly meant was that the Roman Empire, in spite of claiming absolute political dominion, had no dominion over the essential identity of Jesus. By extension, the state has no dominion over any of us. Of course, we may not know this. So we may fear the state, which claims for itself a monopoly on the justified use of violence, which can be used to threaten, imprison, and even destroy our bodies. But if we accept the resurrection belief, we know that the state cannot destroy our essential identity, so that the state has no power over us. As the book of Hebrews, quoting Psalm 118, put it: "The Lord is my helper; I will not be afraid. What can anyone do to me?" (13:6)

Resurrection belief can, it should be added, take many possible forms. Although the term "resurrection" has become associated with the idea of the resurrection of the physical body, the apostle Paul rather clearly rejected this idea in favor of the idea that it is a "spiritual body" that is raised.[13] According to New Testament scholar Gregory Riley, moreover, even the language of "resurrection of the body" appeared rather late, many decades after the event. The first Christians, he says, spoke instead of the "resurrection of the soul"[14] —a phrase that, incidentally, has been proposed by John Cobb.[15]

By extension, moreover, the term resurrection belief can be extended to forms of belief in life after death or immortality that appear in other religions, such as Buddhism and Hinduism. These various forms of resurrection belief are, incidentally, supported by considerable empirical evidence.[16] The term "resurrection" is, to be sure, not normally applied to these alternative forms of belief in life after death or immortality. But these beliefs contain the same central point, namely that our essential identity is not destroyed by the death of our bodies.

This belief was surely crucial for the early survival and growth of the church in the face of hostility from the empire. This hostility was inevitable, because Rome had elevated its emperor to the status of deity, as shown by an inscription about Augustus Caesar, which said:

> The most divine Caesar . . . we should consider equal to the Beginning of all things . . . [t]he beginning of life and vitality . . . who being sent to us and our descendants as Savior, has . . . become [god] manifest. . . . [T]he birthday of the god has been for the whole world the beginning of good news (*euangelion*).[17]

Later Roman emperors were described in similar terms.

From the perspective of Christians, of course, this was idolatry. Christians could *not* profess their allegiance to the Roman emperor. This meant, among other things, that they could not render military service for the empire.

For this and other reasons, Christians became persecuted. Some Christians, of course, recanted their faith. But many remained steadfast, knowing that the empire had no ultimate authority over them. Because of their fearlessness, the persecutions, rather than stamping out the church, helped it grow, as indicated in the famous dictum, "The blood of the martyrs is the seed of the church."

I recall discussing these early Christians martyrs one night at high-school church camp. While we were sitting around the campfire, one girl said, "In a way those early Christians were lucky. It was dangerous to be a Christian then, so they had a chance to demonstrate their faith. But today being a Christian is not dangerous. I wish it were, so that I could show that I am willing to die for my faith."

That was the Eisenhower era. Most Americans thought of the United States as a Christian nation that liberated the world from Fascist dictators, stood up to atheistic Communism, and generally went around the world doing good. In reality, the American empire was doing all sorts of things that would have appalled us—overthrowing democratically elected governments in Iran and Guatemala, starting a civil war in Indonesia, paying for France's attempt to recolonize Vietnam, then taking over the effort ourselves. But most of us didn't know this. We liked Ike, with his genial smile. We couldn't imagine that the government he headed was doing many nefarious things against which Christians should have been protesting.

But today we know. The Roman Empire as portrayed in the book of Revelation was no more demonic, I suggest, than the American empire. Indeed, given the terrible advances in military weaponry since then, the American empire is *more* demonic, because it is a much greater threat to divine purposes.

Some Americans, to be sure, will protest this application of the term "demonic" to this empire. Even many Americans who know America's policies, as opposed to its cultivated image of itself as the champion of everything good and holy, may feel that the description of it as *demonic* goes too far. However, this term surely should be used for *that which is diametrically opposed to divine values and powerful enough to threaten divine purposes.* If we agree that anything fitting this description should be called *demonic*, what other term can be used for a state that seeks to impose its will on the entire world, that oversees a system of global economic control that kills more people every decade than were killed by Hitler and Stalin combined, that refuses to eliminate the threat of nuclear holocaust, and that refuses to take action to reduce the likelihood that human civilization will be brought to an end by global warming within the present century? If such a state should not be called *demonic*, then nothing should.

In any case, I have no idea what became of that girl who wished that it was now dangerous to be a Christian. But if I were to meet up with her again, I would be tempted to remind her of the old adage, Be careful what you wish for! For if we Christians were responding to our country's imperialist policies as we should be, I am afraid that we would very quickly be forced to decide whether we were willing to risk death for our faith—just as Martin Luther King Jr. had to face this question when he started speaking out against the most obviously evil manifestation of American imperialism in his day, the war in Vietnam.

It is time for Christians in America, I believe, to consider whether the situation created by American imperialism creates a *status confessionis*, a confessional situation. In the twentieth century, Nazism and South African apartheid led to such situations.

In Germany in 1934, a year after the Nazi Party's rise to power, the movement known as the *Deutsche Christen*—the "German Christians"—believed that the program of the National Socialists would bring Germany the greatness that it deserved. So they supported the Nazi program. But a number of theologians, led by Karl Barth and Dietrich Bonhoeffer, led a movement of Confessing Christians who said, in their famous Barmen Declaration, that this support for National Socialism violated basic principles of the Christian faith, thereby creating a confessional situation.

Later in the century, some Christian bodies decided that the system of apartheid in South Africa could not remain a matter of indifference. One such body was the Lutheran World Federation. "Under normal circumstances," it declared in 1977, "Christians may have different opinions in political questions." But the system of apartheid in South Africa, it declared, is "so perverted and oppressive" that this situation "constitutes a *status confessionis*." The Christian faith required, therefore, that "churches would publicly and unequivocally reject the existing apartheid system."[18]

I believe that it is time for Christians, both in America and around the world, to engage in an extensive examination of the nature of America's foreign policy to see if it is "so perverted and oppressive" that Christians, individually and as churches, should "publicly and unequivocally" reject it.

I believe it *is* this perverted and oppressive. Let me give one example, drawing on John 21:17. In this passage, the resurrected Jesus says that if Peter truly loves him, Peter will feed his sheep. We can take the voice of the resurrected Jesus here to be the voice of God. If you truly love me, God says, you will feed my sheep. God is, of course, the creator and lover of all people, so *all* people are God's sheep.

In today's world, however, some fifteen million people, most of them children, die every year because of insufficient food and drinking water. Since the end of World War II, the global economy has been presided over by the United

States. And during this period, the gap between the haves and the have-nots of the world has increased greatly. This gap is, in fact, now widely called "global apartheid," with critics pointing out that it is even worse, by every measure, than was apartheid in South Africa.[19] This increasing gap is, furthermore, due primarily to policies deliberately adopted by our government.

In this regard, we cannot remind ourselves too often of the notorious State Department memo written in 1947 by George Kennan, who was in charge of long-range planning. "We have about 50% of the world's wealth, but only 6.3% of its population," Kennan pointed out. He then said, "Our real task in the coming period is to devise a pattern of relationships which will permit us to maintain this position of disparity without positive detriment to our national security."[20] In our present circumstances, it may be the final sentence that grabs our attention, because U.S. foreign policy *has* in recent years resulted in positive detriment to our security—both to us as a nation and to us as individual Americans. For our present purposes, however, the main point is that at a time when our country, with only about 6 percent of the world's population, had about 50 percent of the world's wealth, Kennan said that our foreign policy should be oriented around maintaining this disparity. It is to a large extent because of this general policy that we now have ever increasing global apartheid, with 15 million people dying every year—150 million dying every decade—because of poverty, while the number of billionaires increases.

There is, in other words, a direct connection between the deaths of millions of people every year from starvation and lack of clean drinking water and policies intended to enlarge America's military-economic empire. Since we are commanded to feed God's sheep, this connection by itself should be sufficient reason to make rejection of America's imperialist policies a matter of faith. If the apartheid system in South Africa was "so perverted and oppressive" as to require churches and individual Christians to renounce this system publicly and unequivocally, can anything less be required in relation to the system of *global* apartheid, which by every measure is worse than the apartheid in South Africa? There can, moreover, be no meaningful renunciation of this system without rejecting the imperialistic policies that produce it.

However, although that by itself should provide sufficient reason for Christians to make the stance toward the American empire a matter of faith, it is far from the only reason. At least near the top of the list must be the fact that American leaders are now engaged in what Richard Falk calls the "global domination project," which involves using a combination of economic and, increasingly, military power to bring the whole world under U.S. control. I do not see how we could fail to regard this project—like the Nazi project—as wholly antithetical to Christian faith.

Concluding Thought

For Christians in this country to denounce and work against the American empire will, of course, require courage, because we may be subjected to one of the many contemporary forms of crucifixion. It is good, therefore, that we have our resurrection faith.

Notes

PREFACE

1. Quoted and discussed in Ray McGovern, "God on Their Side," TomPaine.com, December 30, 2003 (*http://www.tompaine.com/feature2.cfm/ID/9678/view/print*).

CHAPTER 1: AMERICA'S NON-ACCIDENTAL, NON-BENIGN EMPIRE

1. Ronald Reagan, "Remarks at the Annual Washington Conference of the American Legion," February 22, 1983; quoted in Andrew J. Bacevich, *The New American Militarism: How Americans Are Seduced by War* (Oxford: Oxford University Press, 2005), 185.

2. Ludwell Denny, *America Conquers Britain* (1930), cited in Titus Alexander, *Unraveling Global Apartheid: An Overview of World Politics* (Cambridge: Polity, 1996), 148.

3. Ernest R. May, *Imperial Democracy: The Emergence of America as a Great Power* (New York: Harcourt, Brace, & World, 1961), 270; quoted in Andrew J. Bacevich, *American Empire: The Realities and Consequences of U.S. Diplomacy* (Cambridge: Harvard University Press, 2002), 7.

4. Ronald Steel, *Pax Americana* (New York: Viking Press, 1967), 15, 14.

5. Ibid., 16–17, 18.

6. Ibid., vii. When I first encountered these statements, I assumed that they were made with tongue in cheek. But Steel clearly meant them. In the meantime, however, he has developed a very different attitude towards the American empire, as evident in his *Temptations of a Superpower* (Cambridge: Harvard University Press, 1995).

7. See David E. Stannard, *American Holocaust: The Conquest of the New World* (New York: Oxford University Press, 1992), 267–68; Francis Jennings, *The Founders of America: From the Earliest Migration to the Present* (New York: Norton, 1993), 395.

8. See Stannard, *American Holocaust*, 317. I reached the estimate of ten million by extrapolating from Stannard's figures for all of the Americas.

9. See Richard W. Van Alstyne, *The Rising America Empire* (1960; New York: Norton, 1974).

10. See Walter LaFeber, *Inevitable Revolutions: The United States in Central America*, 2nd ed. (New York: Norton, 1993).

11. Philip S. Foner, *The Spanish-Cuban-American War and the Birth of American Imperialism*, 2 vols. (New York: Monthly Review, 1972); Stuart Creighton Miller, *"Benevolent Assimilation": The American Conquest of the Philippines, 1899–1903* (New Haven, CT: Yale University Press, 1982).

12. On many of the leading members of the Anti-Imperialist League, see Robert Beisner, *Twelve against Empire: The Anti-Imperialists, 1898–1902* (New York: McGraw-Hill, 1968).

For the writings of one of its prominent members, see Jim Zwick, ed., *Mark Twain's Weapons of Satire: Anti-Imperialist Writings on the Philippine-American War* (Syracuse, NY: Syracuse University Press, 1992).

13. See Lloyd C. Gardner, Walter F. LaFeber, and Thomas J. McCormick, *Creation of the American Empire* (Chicago: Rand McNally, 1973), and Walter LaFeber, Richard Polenberg, and Nancy Woloch, *The American Century: A History of the United States*, 5th ed. (Boston: McGraw-Hill, 1998).

14. See Walter LaFeber, *Inevitable Revolutions* and also *The Panama Canal: The Crisis in Historical Perspective* (New York: Oxford University Press, 1978).

15. See Laurence Shoup and William Minter, *Imperial Brain Trust: The Council on Foreign Relations and United States Foreign Policy* (New York: Monthly Review Press, 1977); David F. Schmitz, *Thank God They're on Our Side: The United States and Right-Wing Dictatorships, 1921–1965* (Chapel Hill: University of North Carolina Press, 1999); Gabriel Kolko, *The Politics of War: The World and United States Foreign Policy 1943–1945* (New York: Pantheon, 1968, 1990), and *Confronting the Third World: United States Foreign Policy 1945–1980* (New York: Pantheon, 1988).

16. See Kolko, *The Politics of War*; Walter LaFeber, *America, Russia, and the Cold War: 1945–1990*, 6th ed. (New York: McGraw-Hill, 1990); Melvin Leffler, *A Preponderance of Power* (Stanford, CA: Stanford University Press, 1992); and Carolyn Eisenberg, *Drawing the Line: The American Decision to Divide Germany, 1944–1949* (Cambridge: Cambridge University Press, 1996).

17. See Schmitz, *Thank God They're on Our Side*; William Blum, *Killing Hope: U.S. Military and CIA Interventions since World War II* (Monroe, ME: Common Courage, 1995); Noam Chomsky, *Year 501: The Conquest Continues* (Boston: South End, 1993); Jonathan Kwitny, *Endless Enemies: The Making of an Unfriendly World* (New York: Penguin Books, 1986); Piero Gleijeses, *Shattered Hope: The Guatemalan Revolution and the United States, 1944–1954* (Princeton, NJ: Princeton University Press, 1991); Peter Kornbluh, *Nicaragua: The Price of Intervention: Reagan's Wars against the Sandinistas* (Washington, DC: Institute for Policy Studies, 1987); and LaFeber, *Inevitable Revolutions*.

18. See George McT. Kahin, *Intervention: How America Became Involved in Vietnam* (New York: Anchor, 1987), and Marilyn B. Young, *The Vietnam Wars: 1945–1990* (New York: HarperPerennial, 1991).

19. See Noam Chomsky, *Fateful Triangle: The United States, Israel, and the Palestinians*, updated ed., foreword by Edward Said (Cambridge, MA: South End, 1999); Charles D. Smith, *Palestine and the Arab-Israeli Conflict: A History with Documents*, 4th ed. (Boston: Bedford/St. Martin's, 2001); Phyllis Bennis, *Before and After: US Foreign Policy and the September 11th Crisis* (New York: Olive Branch, 2003); Richard Labevière, *Dollars for Terror: The United States and Islam* (New York: Algora, 2000); Eqbal Ahmad, *Terrorism: Theirs and Ours* (New York: Seven Stories, 2001); John K. Cooley, *Unholy Wars: Afghanistan, America and International Terrorism*, 2nd ed. (London: Pluto, 2000); Dilip Hiro, *Iraq: In the Eye of the Storm* (New York: Nation Books, 2002).

20. See Robert J. Lifton and Richard Falk, *Indefensible Weapons: The Political and Psychological Case against Nuclearism* (New York: Basic Books, 1982); Francis A. Boyle, *The Criminality of Nuclear Deterrence: Could the U.S. War on Terrorism Go Nuclear?* (Atlanta: Clarity Press, 2002); and Helen Caldicott, *The New Nuclear Danger: George W. Bush's Military-Industrial Complex* (New York: New York Press, 2002).

21. Andrew J. Bacevich, *American Empire*.

22. See Richard W. Van Alstyne, *The Rising American Empire* (1960; New York: Norton, 1974); Noam Chomsky, *American Power and the New Mandarins* (1967; New York: Vintage Books, 1969), and *Rogue States: The Rule of Force in World Affairs* (Cambridge: South End Press, 2000); Richard Falk, "Imperialism in Crisis," an introduction to Mansour Farhang, *U.S. Imperialism: From the Spanish-American War to the Iranian Revolution* (Boston: South End Press, 1981); Lloyd C. Gardner, Walter F. LaFeber, and Thomas J. McCormick, *Creation of the American Empire* (1973); Walter LaFeber, *The New Empire: An Interpretation of American Expansion 1860–1898* (1963; Ithaca, NY: Cornell University Press, 1998); Harry Magdoff, *The Age of Imperialism: The Economics of U.S. Foreign Policy* (New York: Monthly Review, 1966, 1969); Thomas J. McCormick, *China Market: America's Quest for Informal Empire, 1893–1901* (Chicago: Quadrangle Books, 1967); Michael Parenti, *Against Empire* (San Francisco: City Lights, 1995); Laurence Shoup and William Minter, *Imperial Brain Trust: The Council on Foreign Relations and United States Foreign Policy* (New York: Monthly Review Press, 1977); William Appleton Williams, *The Tragedy of American Diplomacy* (1959; New York: Norton, 1988), and *Empire as a Way of Life: An Essay on the Causes and Character of America's Present Predicament* (Oxford: Oxford University Press, 1980); and Howard Zinn, *A People's History of the United States* (New York: Harper, 1980, 1990).

23. Remarks by the President at 2002 Graduation Exercise of the United States Military Academy, June 1, 2002 (*http://www.whitehouse.gov/news/releases/2002/06/20020601–3.html*); Department of Defense press conference, April 23, 2003, quoted in Rahul Mahajan, *Full Spectrum Dominance: U.S. Power in Iraq and Beyond* (New York: Seven Stories Press, 2003), 9.

24. Quoted in Bacevich, *American Empire*, 219. Haass, to be sure, paid deference to the long-standing distaste for "imperialism" by adding: "An imperial foreign policy is not to be confused with imperialism." But he probably realized that this is a distinction without a difference.

25. Robert Kagan, "The Clinton Legacy Abroad," *Weekly Standard*, January 15, 2001; quoted in Bacevich, *The New American Militarism*, 85.

26. Krauthammer's statements, originally published in Emily Eakin, "All Roads Lead to D.C.," *New York Times*, Week In Review, March 31, 2002, are quoted in Jonathan Freedland, "Is America the New Rome?" *Guardian*, Sept. 18, 2002, G2: 2–5.

27. Bacevich, *American Empire*, 243–44.

28. Robert Kaplan, "Supremacy by Stealth: Ten Rules for Managing the World," *Atlantic Monthly*, July/August, 2003.

29. Richard Perle, "Thank God for the Death of the UN," *Guardian*, March 21, 2003.

30. Bacevich, *American Empire*, 7.

31. May, *Imperial Democracy*, 270; quoted in Bacevich, *American Empire*, 7.

32. Bacevich, *American Empire*, 7.

33. Ibid., viii.

34. Ibid., 127.

35. Ibid., viii.

36. Ibid., 14–17.

37. Ibid., 30. This quotation is Bacevich's summary of the position of Williams.

38. Ibid., ix, 6.

39. Richard Van Alstyne, *The Rising American Empire*, vii.

40. Anders Stephanson, *Manifest Destiny: American Expansion and the Empire of Right* (New York: Hill & Wang, 1995), 19.

41. Stephanson, *Manifest Destiny*, xi.

42. Van Alstyne, *The Rising American Empire*, 159.

43. Stephanson, *Manifest Destiny*, 90.

44. Charles Krauthammer, "The Unipolar Moment," *Foreign Affairs* 70/1 (1990–91): 295–306, at 304–5.

45. Robert Kagan, "The Benevolent Empire," *Foreign Policy*, Summer 1998: 24–35.

46. Dinesh D'Souza, "In Praise of an American Empire," *Christian Science Monitor*, April 26, 2002.

47. Charles Krauthammer, "The Unipolar Era," in Andrew J. Bacevich, ed., *The Imperial Tense: Prospects and Problems of American Empire* (Chicago: Ivan R. Dee, 2003), 47–65, at 59. This track record, he says, proves that "the United States is not an imperial power with a desire to rule other countries." (This essay was originally published in the Winter 2003 issue of *The National Interest*.)

48. Michael Ignatieff, "The American Empire: The Burden," *New York Times Magazine*, January 5, 2003: 23–27, 50–54, at 24, 52.

49. Charles Krauthammer, "Tomorrow's Threat," *Washington Post*, January 21, 2005.

50. "Inaugural Address by George W. Bush," *New York Times*, January 20, 2005 (*http://www.nytimes.com/2005/01/20/politics/20BUSH-TEXT.html*).

51. Bacevich, *American Empire*, 7.

52. Ibid., 46.

53. Ibid., 4, 133.

54. Ibid., 52.

55. Ibid., 115, 196.

56. Noam Chomsky, *Deterring Democracy*, 2nd ed. (New York: Hill & Wang, 1992).

57. Jonathan Freedland, "Is America the New Rome?"

58. Charles Krauthammer, "The Bush Doctrine," *Time*, March 5, 2001, quoted in Chalmers Johnson, *The Sorrows of Empire: Militarism, Secrecy, and the End of the Republic* (New York: Henry Holt [Metropolitan Books], 2004), 68.

59. Bacevich, *American Empire*, 242 (quoting Charles Beard, *Giddy Minds and Foreign Quarrels* [1939], 87).

60. Bacevich, *American Empire*, 244, 244.

61. Richard A. Horsley, *Jesus and Empire: The Kingdom of God and the New World Disorder* (Minneapolis: Fortress, 2003), 197.

62. Tacitus, *Agricola* 14.1; quoted in Horsley, *Jesus and Empire*, 31.

63. Susan P. Mattern, *Rome and the Enemy: Imperial Strategy in the Principate* (Berkeley: University of California Press, 1999), 117, 172.

64. Colin Powell, testimony to the U.S. Congress, 1992.

65. Bacevich, *American Empire*, 44.

66. Ibid., 44–45.

67. *The National Security Strategy of the United States of America*, September 2002 (available at *www.whitehouse.gov/nsc/nss.html*), 29–30, 6.

68. *Rebuilding America's Defenses: Strategy, Forces, and Resources for a New Century*, A Report of the Project for the New American Century, September 2000 (www.newamericancentury .org).

69. General Howell M. Estes III, USAF, United States Space Command, "Vision for 2020," February 1997 (http://www.fas.org/spp/military/docops/usspac/visbook.pdf). This document begins by saying: "During the rise of sea commerce, nations built navies to protect and enhance their commercial interests. During the westward expansion of the continental

United States, military outposts and the cavalry emerged to protect our wagon trains, settlements, and railroads. The emergence of space power follows both of these models. Over the past several decades, space power has primarily supported land, sea, and air operations . . . . During the early portion of the 21st century, space power will also evolve into a separate and equal medium of warfare. The medium of space is the fourth medium of warfare—along with land, sea, and air. Space power . . . will be increasingly leveraged to close the ever-widening gap between diminishing resources and increasing military commitments. . . . The emerging synergy of space superiority with land, sea, and air superiority, will lead to Full Spectrum Dominance."

70. This is, of course, not a divergence from prior policy. See, for example, the quotation from George Kennan in chapter 9.

71. The developments achieved already by 1998 are described in George Friedman and Meredith Friedman, *The Future of War: Power, Technology, and American World Dominance in the 21st Century* (New York: St. Martin's, 1998).

72. Hitt, "The Next Battlefield May Be in Outer Space."

73. Tim Weiner, "Air Force Seeks Bush's Approval for Space Weapons Programs," *New York Times*, May 18, 2005 (*http://www.nytimes.com/2005/05/18/business/18space.html?th& emc=th*).

74. Hitt, "The Next Battlefield May Be in Outer Space." For a brief overview of this project, see Karl Grossman's *Weapons in Space*.

75. Rahul Mahajan, *Full Spectrum Dominance*, 53–54, quoting *Rebuilding America's Defenses*, 54.

76. Condoleezza Rice, "Remarks on Foreign Policy Issues," November 16, 2000; Lawrence Kaplan, *New Republic* 224 (March 12, 2001), cover text; both quoted in Bacevich, *American Empire*, 223.

77. See "Resisting the Global Domination Project: An Interview with Prof. Richard Falk," *Frontline* 20/8 (April 12–25, 2003), and Falk's *The Great Terror War* (New York: Olive Branch Press, 2002), xxvii.

78. See Robert Brank Fulton, *Adam Smith Speaks to Our Times* (Boston: Christopher House, 1963), 388–89.

79. *Rebuilding America's Defenses*, 51. This apparent hope for a "new Pearl Harbor" had already been articulated in Zbigniew Brzezinski's *The Grand Chessboard: American Primacy and Its Geostrategic Imperatives* (New York: Basic Books, 1997), as can be seen by reading pages 24–25 together with page 212.

80. *Report of the Commission to Assess U.S. National Security Space Management and Organization* (www.defenselink.mil/cgi-bin/dlprint.cgi).

81. This according to the *Washington Post*, Jan. 27, 2002.

82. Henry Kissinger, "Destroy the Network," *Washington Post*, Sept. 11, 2001 (http:// washingtonpost.com), quoted in Thierry Meyssan, *9:11: The Big Lie* (London: Carnot, 2002), 65; Lance Morrow, "The Case for Rage and Retribution," *Time*, Sept. 11, 2001.

83. "Secretary Rumsfeld Interview with the *New York Times*," *New York Times*, October 12, 2001. For Rice's statement, see Chalmers Johnson, *The Sorrows of Empire: Militarism, Secrecy, and the End of the Republic* (New York: Henry Holt, 2004), 229.

84. Bob Woodward, *Bush at War* (New York: Simon & Schuster, 2002), 32.

85. *The National Security Strategy of the United States of America*.

86. Johnson, *The Sorrows of Empire*, 33, 4.

87. Bacevich, *American Empire*, 298.

88. Bacevich, *The New American Militarism*, 54.

89. Ibid., 4–6.

90. Ibid., 2, 3, 7.

91. Ibid., 147.

92. Ibid., 72. For the efforts of the neoconservatives with regard to the doctrines of regime change and preventive war, see ibid., 85–86, 90,

93. Ibid., 80, quoting Gary Dorrien, *The Neoconservative Mind: Politics, Culture, and the War of Ideology* (Philadelphia: Temple University Press, 1993), 117, who quoted Kristol's statement from the *Wall Street Journal*, March 3, 1986.

94. Bacevich, *The New American Militarism*, 83.

95. Ibid., quoting Robert Kagan, "American Power—A Guide for the Perplexed," *Commentary* 101 (April 1996).

96. Bacevich, *The New American Militarism*, 85.

97. Ibid., 17.

98. Ibid., 19.

99. Ibid., 241 n. 99; citing an open letter from William Kristol et al., Project for the New American Century, to George W. Bush, January 23, 2003.

100. Bacevich, *The New American Militarism*, 17 and 229 n. 17. Bacevich is citing Bruce Berkowitz, *The New Face of War: How War Will Be Fought in the 21st Century* (New York: Free Press, 2003), 4.

101. Jurgen Brauer and Nicholas Anglewicz, "Two-Thirds On Defense," Tom Paine, June 10, 2005 (*http://www.tompaine.com/articles/20050610/twothirds_on_defense.php*). The percentage remains roughly the same because the BEA figure also did not include the interest paid on the part of the debt not caused by military spending. (Brauer is the senior author of this article; Nicholas Anglewicz is an MBA student at Augusta State University in Augusta, Georgia, where Brauer teaches economics.)

102. Bacevich, *The New American Militarism*, 146.

103. David Ray Griffin, *The New Pearl Harbor: Disturbing Questions about the Bush Administration and 9/11* (Northampton, MA: Interlink, 2004), xxiii.

104. The final report of the 9/11 Commission says that the "professional staff, headed by Philip Zelikow, . . . conducted the exacting investigative work upon which the Commission has built" (*The 9/11 Commission Report: Final Report of the National Commission on Terrorist Attacks upon the United States*, authorized edition [New York: W. W. Norton, 2004], xvi–xvii).

105. Zelikow worked with Condoleezza Rice on the National Security Council in the George H. W. Bush administration, after which he coauthored a book with her. She then, as national security advisor for George W. Bush, had Zelikow help set up the new National Security Council, after which he was appointed by Bush to the president's Foreign Intelligence Advisory Board. Rice then, after being appointed secretary of state in the second term of this administration, brought him into the State Department.

106. David Ray Griffin, *The 9/11 Commission Report: Omissions and Distortions* (Northampton, MA: Olive Branch [Interlink Books], 2005), 19–20.

107. Ibid., 20–21.

108. Ibid., 25–27.

109. Ibid., 26.

110. Ibid., 26–27.

111. Ibid., 33–38.

112. Ibid., 59–60.

113. Ibid., 238–39, 252–53.

114. I have summarized these 115 omission and distortions, treated as two types of lies, in "The 9/11 Commission Report: A 571-Page Lie" (*http://www.septembereleventh.org/newsarchive/2005–05-22–571pglie.php*).

115. Bacevich, *The New American Militarism*, 91.

116. "9/11 and the American Empire: How Should Religious People Respond?" 9/11 Citizens Watch, May 7, 2005 (*http://www.911citizenswatch.org/modules.php?op=modload&name=News&file=article&sid=535*).

CHAPTER 2: IMPERIALISM IN AMERICAN ECONOMIC POLICY

1. See Herman E. Daly and John B. Cobb Jr., *For the Common Good: Redirecting the Economy toward Community, the Environment, and a Sustainable Future*, 2nd ed. (Boston: Beacon Press, 1994), and John B. Cobb Jr., *The Earthist Challenge to Economism: A Theological Critique of the World Bank* (Houndmills, UK: Macmillan, 1999).

2. John Perkins, *Confessions of an Economic Hit Man* (San Francisco: Berrett-Koehler, 2004).

3. For an illuminating account of this history and what follows, see Walden Bello, *Dark Victory: The United States, Structural Adjustment, and Global Poverty* (London: Pluto Press, 1994).

4. I discussed the debt crisis in a chapter entitled "To Pay or Not to Pay" in my *Sustaining the Common Good: A Christian Perspective on the Global Economy* (Cleveland: Pilgrim Press, 1994).

CHAPTER 3: SLOUCHING TOWARD A FASCIST WORLD ORDER

1. Zbigniew Brzezinski, *The Choice: Global Domination or Global Leadership* (New York: Basic Books, 2003), 218.

2. Ibid., xi, 218.

3. In this respect, at least, the candid avowal of an imperial role is to be preferred, as in Niall Ferguson, *Colossus: The Price of America's Empire* (New York: Penguin, 2004).

4. *Rebuilding America's Defenses: Strategy, Forces, and Resources for a New Century*, A Report of the Project for the New American Century, September 2000 (*www.newamericancentury.org*). It should be read in conjunction with David Ray Griffin, *The New Pearl Harbor: Disturbing Questions about the Bush Administration and 9/11*, foreword by Richard Falk (Northampton, MA: Interlink, 2004).

5. For a consideration of these prospects if the Democratic Party should return to power, see Richard Falk, "Toward a Revival of a Principled American Foreign Policy," *Tikkun Magazine*, 2004.

6. Such attacks could, however, lend support to the Spanish response to the Madrid train attacks of March 11, 2004: "No to war, No to terrorism." The Spanish people voted against the government of Prime Minster José Maria Aznar, which had supported the invasion of Iraq the prior year, and unexpectedly brought to power the Zapatero social democratic leadership, which immediately announced the removal of Spanish troops from Iraq (while affirming its resolve to increase law enforcement efforts against terrorism). There is, however, little sign that this will be the response in America or Britain.

7. I have in mind thinkers such as Andrew Bacevich, Robert Kagan, Michael Ignatieff, and Niall Ferguson. In actuality, this acknowledgment of empire as the defining reality for both American foreign policy and world order in our time exists across the political spectrum of American opinion.

8. For discussion of the complex role of "rogue states" in the bipartisan American effort to mobilize support for its imperial ambitions and their military infrastructure after the Cold War, see Michael Klare, *Rogue States and Nuclear Outlaws* (New York: Hill & Yang, 1995).

9. The nature of the American adversary has become less and less clear since 9/11. It seemed initially accurate to think of a network of cells situated in many countries, with head-quarters in Afghanistan, where the leadership, headed by Osama bin Laden, set policy, endorsed attacks, and provided training and resources. Increasingly, such an image came to seem less illuminating. It even now seems dubious to think of al-Qaeda as a unified political entity or, perhaps, even to regard al-Qaeda as persisting as a political actor. It appears to be more accurate to posit an international jihadist movement, composed of varying groups, drawing inspiration from the general vision and tactics articulated by bin Laden, but also by other leading figures associated with political Islam. For valuable perspectives on political Islam, see Mahmood Mamdani, *Good Muslim, Bad Muslim* (New York: Pantheon, 2004), and Roxanne Euben, *Enemy in My Mirror* (Princeton, NJ: Princeton University Press, 2000).

10. "Treaty on the Non-Proliferation of Nuclear Weapons," which entered into force March 5, 1970 (*http://www.fas.org/nuke/control/npt/text/npt2.htm*).

11. Nuclear weapons on the scale of 5 kilotons are hardly "mini," having about half the destructive capability of the bombs dropped on Hiroshima and Nagasaki, which were estimated at between 10 and 20 kilotons. It should be obvious that a 5-kiloton weapon is an extraordinarily destructive weapon.

12. See Francis Fukuyama, *The End of History and the Last Man* (New York: Penguin, 1992).

13. The Reagan presidency arguably flirted with a nonrealist approach to geopolitics, identifying the Soviet Union as "the evil empire" and seeking to intimidate it by embarking upon a bankrupting arms race, including a Star Wars scenario with offensive possibilities for mounting a first strike. Such an approach, which abandons the geopolitical virtue of prudence, was viewed with alarm by many citizens, especially in western Europe, giving rise to the first large-scale transnational peace movements and the idea of civil society as an agent of change in global policy. See, for instance, Mary Kaldor, Gerald Holden, and Richard Falk, eds., *The New Détente: Rethinking East-West Relations* (London and New York: Verso, 1989).

14. For the most influential statement of this perspective, see Hedley Bull, *The Anarchical Society* (New York: Columbia University Press, 1977). For a recent statement, see Robert Jackson, *The Global Covenant: Human Conduct in a World of States* (Oxford: Oxford University Press, 2000).

15. Al-Qaeda, by contrast, can be understood as an expression of the corrupting impact of *powerlessness*, prompting massive violence against civilian innocence. Policy analysts speak of "asymmetric warfare," implying that the violence of the weak requires different approaches, so that military and political capabilities must be readjusted. Part of this readjustment is evident in the rewriting of international law, the redefinition of the word "torture," and the reliance on special forces for a variety of undisclosed dirty missions inside foreign countries, with or without the permission of the territorial government.

16. *The National Security Strategy of the United States of America*, September 2002 (*www.whitehouse.gov/nsc/nss.html*); "Remarks by the President at 2002 Graduation Exercise of the United States Military Academy," June 1, 2002 (*http://www.whitehouse.gov/news/releases/2002/06/20020601–3.html*).

17. For some earlier speculation along these lines, see Richard Falk, "Will the Empire Be Fascist?" *Global Dialogues*, 2003.

18. I refer to a work in progress by Griffin on global democracy.

19. To the extent that European and Japanese elite opinion accepts the soft option of American global empire, it may also reflect "free rider" benefits accruing to rich countries in the face of growing scarcities.

20. Signs of impending unpleasantness include expressions of regret for such developments while arguing for their necessity. For a prime example, see Michael Ignatieff, *The Lesser of Evils: Political Ethics in an Age of Terror* (Princeton, NJ: Princeton University Press, 2004). In this instance, a prominent author, who is director of the Carr Center of Human Rights at Harvard, is providing leaders with excuses for every intrusion on individuals' rights, even for torture. Already, the climate induced by 9/11 is giving respectability and prime-time media access to opportunistic scoundrels.

21. There are some liberal proponents of a solution to the challenge of global governance by more consensual means. See, for instance, Anne-Marie Slaughter, *A New World Order* (Princeton, NJ: Princeton University Press, 2004), and Amitai Etzioni, *From Empire to Community: A New Approach to International Relations* (New York: Palgrave Macmillan, 2004).

22. For an early attempt to portray this response, which I now only partly endorse, see Falk, *The Great Terror War* (Northampton, MA: Interlink, 2003).

23. Michael Ignatieff, "The Burden," *New York Times Magazine*, Jan. 5, 2003: 23–27, 50–54.

24. See Richard Falk, "Toward a Revival of a Principled American Foreign Policy," *Tikkun Magazine*, 2004.

25. For an example of an excellent account of fascism, see Robert O. Paxton, *The Anatomy of Fascism* (New York: Knopf, 2004).

26. For this neocon worldview, see David Frum and Richard Perle, *An End to Evil: How to Win the War on Terror* (New York: Random House, 2003).

27. Davos, Switzerland, is where the World Economic Forum is held. For a brief account, see the second section of Cobb's second essay in this volume, p. 90.

CHAPTER 4: RENOUNCING WARS OF CHOICE: TOWARD A GEOPOLITICS OF NONVIOLENCE

1. There are variations with respect to degrees of war-proneness. Europe, after enduring centuries of internal warfare and projecting its power globally by reliance on the superiority of its war-fighting abilities, seems to have evolved toward a greater willingness to rely on international law and peaceful procedures for conflict resolution. It may yet induce other actors and regions to move away from the war system.

2. The argument against war is more complex, but no less convincing, if it is admitted, as I discussed in the previous chapter, that supposedly defensive wars are often undertaken largely, if not exclusively, to achieve strategic goals of expansion, influence, and domination. The Iraq War is best explained as a strategic war fought to exert greater control over the Middle East, not as an antiterrorist war fought, for example, to protect the American people from future terrorist attacks.

3. This conclusion has been reached by a wide variety of international law specialists. See the 2004 plenary panel at the American Society of International Law (ASIL), "Iraq One Year After," published in the 2004 Proceedings of the ASIL, which includes presentations by Mary-Ellen O'Connell, Anne-Marie Slaughter, Thomas Franck, James Crawford, and Richard Falk.

4. I offer such an assessment in preliminary form in Falk, *The Great Terror War* (Northampton, MA: Interlink, 2003).

5. This view was set forth authoritatively by Hedley Bull in *The Anarchical Society* (New York: Columbia University Press, 1977).

6. I have discussed this situation in *Declining World Order: America's Imperial Geopolitics* (New York: Routledge, 2004).

7. This view has been unabashedly articulated by two neocon insiders, David Frum and Richard Perle, in *An End to Evil: How to Win the War on Terror* (New York: Random House, 2003).

8. *National Security Strategy of the United States of America*, September 2002 (*www.whitehouse.gov/nsc/nss.html*).

9. This analysis was persuasively made by Jonathan Schell, *The Fate of the Earth* (New York: Knopf, 1982). More recently, Robert McNamara in a film, *The Fog of War*, reminds us how fortunate we were to have avoided some version of this tragedy, particularly in the setting of the Cuban Missile Crisis in 1962, when leaders on both sides came frighteningly close to embarking upon nuclear warfare.

10. One concerted effort to offer such an alternative vision was in the form of a revamped United Nations, reconfigured as a war-prevention mechanism. See Grenville Clark and Louis B. Sohn, *World Peace through World Law*, 3rd ed. (Cambridge: Harvard University Press, 1966). For a transnational attempt to project feasible utopias, see the publications of the World Order Models Project. This overall perspective is set forth in Saul H. Mendlovitz, ed., *Towards a Just World Order* (New York: Free Press, 1975).

11. I have argued this case more fully in *The Declining World Order*.

12. World government has long been advocated as a coherent response, but this advocacy has generally been unaccompanied by a politics of transition, showing how it would be possible to get from here to there. This apolitical conception of world government has given such thinking a bad name, making "utopian" a word of opprobrium. This is unfortunate, because we need to encourage radical thinking to overcome the deep crisis of world order as conceived from Westphalian perspectives.

13. Mohamad Mahathir, address to the leaders of the Non-Aligned Movement, Kuala Lumpur, Malaysia, Feb. 24, 2003.

14. Jonathan Schell, *The Unconquerable World: Power, Nonviolence, and the Will of the People* (New York: Metropolitan Books, 2003).

15. For a notable attempt along these lines, see Fred Dallmayr, *Peace Talks: Who Will Listen?* (Notre Dame, IN: Notre Dame University Press, 2004).

CHAPTER 6: GLOBAL EMPIRE OR GLOBAL DEMOCRACY: THE PRESENT CHOICE

1. Andrew Bard Schmookler, *The Parable of the Tribes: The Problem of Power in Social Evolution* (Boston: Houghton Mifflin, 1986).

2. Ibid., 21–22.

3. Ibid., 45. Schmookler's point here is supported by Gerda Lerner's observation that non-hierarchical societies, for the most part, simply did not survive. See Lerner's *The Creation of Patriarchy* (New York: Oxford University Press, 1986), 35.

4. Michael E. Brown, Sean M. Lynn-Jones, and Steven E. Miller, eds., *The Perils of Anarchy: Contemporary Realism and International Security* (Cambridge, MA: MIT Press, 1995), ix.

5. David Held, *Democracy and the Global Order: From the Modern State to Cosmopolitan Governance* (Stanford, CA: Stanford University Press, 1995), 74–75.

6. These statements from Thucydides are quoted in Schmookler, *The Parable of the Tribes*, 70.

7. Kenneth N. Waltz, *Man, the State, and War: A Theoretical Analysis* (New York: Columbia University Press, 1959), 231–33.

8. Hidemi Suganami, *On the Causes of War* (Oxford: Clarendon, 1996).

9. Schmookler, *The Parable of the Tribes*, 22–24.

10. John Herz, having spoken of "the security dilemma" in 1951, has restated it in *The Nation State and the Crisis of World Politics* (New York: David McKay, 1976), 9–10.

11. Schmookler, *The Parable of the Tribes*, 24.

12. Ibid., 33, 87, 282.

13. William H. McNeill, *The Pursuit of Power: Technology, Armed Force, and Society since A.D. 1000* (Chicago: University of Chicago Press, 1982), 383–84.

14. Waltz, *Man, the State, and War*, 228, 238.

15. David Gauthier, *The Logic of Leviathan: The Moral and Political Theory of Thomas Hobbes* (Oxford: Clarendon, 1969), 207–11.

16. G. Lowes Dickenson, *The International Anarchy, 1904–1915* (London: Allen & Unwin, 1926). According to Hedley Bull (*The Anarchical Society: A Study of Order in World Politics* [London: Macmillan, 1977], 46), it was Dickenson's book that made the phrase "international anarchy" commonplace.

17. For well-informed arguments for global government by two political realists who were well known in their day, see Frederick L. Schuman, *The Commonwealth of Man: An Inquiry into Power Politics and World Government* (London: Robert Hale, 1954), and Georg Schwarzenberger, *Power Politics: A Study of World Society*, 3rd ed. (London: Stevens, 1964). For well-crafted arguments on behalf of global government from more recent realists, see James P. Speer, *World Polity: Conflict and War: History Causes, Consequences, Cures* (Fort Bragg, CA: Q.E.D. Press, 1986), and two books by Ronald Glossop: *Confronting War: An Examination of Humanity's Most Pressing Problem*, 3rd ed. (Jefferson, NC: McFarland, 1995), and *World Federation? A Critical Analysis of Federal World Government* (Jefferson, NC: McFarland, 1993). For an excellent book in which world government is advocated on the basis of a historical study of the idea, see Cornelius F. Murphy Jr., *Theories of World Governance: A Study in the History of Ideas* (Washington, DC: Catholic University of America Press, 1999).

18. In a more extensive analysis, I would need to add the clarification made in the text at the location of notes 7 and 8 that although there are several permissive causes, international anarchy is the only one that could be eliminated.

19. James P. Speer, *World Polity*, 152.

20. Richard Perle, "Thank God for the Death of the UN," *Guardian*, March 21, 2003.

21. Charles Krauthammer, "The Unipolar Moment," *Foreign Affairs* 70 (1990): 25.

22. Lawrence Kaplan and William Kristol, *The War over Iraq: Saddam's Tyranny and America's Mission* (San Francisco: Encounter Books), 121.

23. Charles Krauthammer, "The Unipolar Era," in Andrew J. Bacevich, ed., *The Imperial Tense: Prospects and Problems of American Empire* (Chicago: Ivan R. Dee, 2003), 47–65, at 59.

24. I am alluding here to the democratic "all-affected principle," according to which all people affected by some policy should have been participants in creating it—a principle that is extremely violated in many ways in today's world.

25. Charles Taliaferro, "God's Natural Laws," in *Natural Law, Liberalism, and Morality: Contemporary Essays*, ed. Robert P. George (Oxford: Clarendon, 1996), 283–301, at 293. Taliaferro has also discussed this theory in "Relativising the Ideal Observer Theory," *Philosophy and Phenomenological Research* 49/1 (1988): 123–38. Other philosophers who have endorsed

the ideal observer account of morality are Richard B. Brandt, *Ethical Theory* (Englewood Cliffs, NJ: Prentice-Hall, 1959), chaps. 7–11; Roderick Firth, "Ethical Absolutism and the Ideal Observer," *Philosophy and Phenomenological Research* 12 (1952): 317–45; and Charles Reynolds, "A Proposal for Understanding the Place of Reason in Christian Ethics," *Journal of Religion* 50/2 (April 1970): 155–68, and "Elements of a Decision Procedure for Christian Social Ethics," *Harvard Theological Review* 65 (1972): 509–30. Not all of these philosophers, I should add, give the ideal observer all three attributes contained in my own presentation.

26. Jürgen Habermas, *Justification and Application: Remarks on Discourse Ethics,* trans. Ciaran Cronin (Cambridge: Polity Press, 1993), 24; emphasis deleted.

27. Habermas, *Justification and Application*, 49; emphasis original.

28. Gilbert Harman, *The Nature of Morality: An Introduction to Ethics* (New York: Oxford University Press, 1977), 49.

29. Reinhold Niebuhr, *Moral Man and Immoral Society: A Study in Ethics and Politics* (Louisville, KY, and London: Westminster John Knox Press, 2001; originally published by Charles Scribner's Sons, 1932). As Niebuhr himself later saw, the complete contrast implied by that title was too strong. But the basic point, as stated in the text, remains valid.

30. Quoted by Fred Pearc in "Earth at the Mercy of National Interests," *New Scientist* 134/1826 (1992): 4.

31. Lord Acton made this statement in an 1887 letter to Bishop Mandell Creighton. It is quoted in Garry Wills, *Papal Sin: Structures of Deceit* (New York: Doubleday, 2000), 2.

32. Niebuhr, *The Children of Light and the Children of Darkness: A Vindication of Democracy and a Critique of Its Traditional Defense* (New York: Scribner's, 1944), xiii.

33. In *The Nature and Destiny of Man* (Louisville, KY, and London: Westminster John Knox Press, 1996; originally published by Charles Scribner's Sons, 1943), 2:249, Niebuhr says: "The capacity of communities to synthesize divergent approaches to a common problem and to arrive at a tolerably just solution proves man's capacity to consider interests other than his own."

34. In *Moral Man and Immoral Society*, Niebuhr famously analyzed the tendency of groups, such as nations, to be even more self-centered than the individuals making them up.

35. *Nature and Destiny of Man*, 2:22.

36. Ibid., 2:29.

37. I have discussed what are, from my perspective, the strengths and weaknesses of Niebuhr's position in an unpublished paper, "The Failure of Modern Religious Realism." In that paper, I seek to explain why Niebuhr, in spite of his initial endorsement of world government (which is reflected in some of my quotations in this chapter), became a strong opponent of it.

38. The notion of "impartiality" should not be equated with "neutrality," which would put this notion of God in tension with God's "preferential option for the poor," rightly emphasized by liberation theologians. Precisely because God's love is impartial, God wants us to overcome those structural injustices within each country and in the world as a whole—constituting what is correctly called "global apartheid"—that cause widespread suffering in a high percentage of the world's people, and thereby in God.

39. Niebuhr, *The Nature and Destiny of Man*, 2:266.

40. *Love and Justice: Selections from the Shorter Writings of Reinhold Niebuhr*, ed. D. B. Robertson (Philadelphia: Westminster, 1957), 248.

41. Support for this project can be found in Pope John XXIII, who said, "Today the universal common good poses problems of world-wide dimension which cannot be adequately

tackled or solved except by the efforts of . . . public authorities which are in a position to operate in an effective manner on a world-wide basis. The moral order itself, therefore, demands
that such a form of public authority be established" (*Pacem in Terris*, part 4).

42. I am making this argument in a book in progress on global democracy.

43. This slogan is gratefully adapted from a similar claim made by Paul and Anne Ehrlich
about population control. Although I agree with their claim, I regard global democracy as the
more inclusive goal.

44. For example, Hans Morgenthau, generally considered the founding father of political
realism in the United States, said that although war could be ended by the creation of a global
government, the precondition for such a government would be a global society with a unifor-
mity in beliefs and values that we will probably not have for another two centuries (*Politics
among Nations: The Struggle for Power and Peace*, 5th ed. [New York: Knopf, 1972]). Kenneth Waltz made the same point in saying that "[t]he amount of force needed to hold a society
together varies with the heterogeneity of the elements composing it" (*Man, the State, and War*,
228), the implication being that there is far too much heterogeneity in the world today for a
global government to be held together without far more coercive force than would be acceptable. And B. V. A. Röling has argued that "[s]tates and peoples differ too much in interests and
in values for 'one world' to be feasible. . . . '[O]ne world' is impossible without an unacceptable dictatorial setting" ("Are Grotius' Ideas Obsolete in an Expanded World?" in *Hugo Grotius
and International Relations,* ed. Hedley Bull, Benedict Kingsbury, and Adam Roberts [Oxford:
Clarendon, 1992], 281–99, at 294). These authors, however, were evidently unaware that a constitution for a global democratic government needs common agreement only on a rather
abstract set of basic principles, which are already implicit in all the traditions.

45. See David Ray Griffin, ed., *Deep Religious Pluralism* (Louisville, KY: Westminster
John Knox, 2005). This volume is based on a conference oriented around the complementary
pluralism pioneered by John B. Cobb Jr., which is expressed in his *Beyond Dialogue: Toward
a Mutual Transformation of Christianity and Buddhism* (Philadelphia: Fortress, 1982) and
Transforming Christianity and the World: A Way beyond Absolutism and Relativism, ed. Paul
F. Knitter (Maryknoll, NY: Orbis, 1999).

46. See note 53, below.

47. On the distinction between moral and "scientific" Marxism, see Alvin W. Gouldner,
The Two Marxisms: Contradictions and Anomalies in the Development of Theory (New York:
Oxford University Press, 1980). In China, this moral Marxism is often called "practical Marx-
ism," in distinction from "scientific" Marxism with its "dialectical materialism." On this, see
"Contemporary Development of Marxist Philosophy in China," *Socialism and Democracy*,
Spring 2001, by Ouyang Kang, one of the China's leading Marxist philosophers.

48. Hans Küng, *A Global Ethic for Global Politics and Economics* (New York: Oxford University Press, 1998), 98–99.

49. Michael Walzer, *Thick and Thin: Moral Argument at Home and Abroad* (Notre Dame,
IN: University of Notre Dame Press, 1994), xi.

50. In my view, it matters not on which term one puts the primary emphasis, as long as
both elements are included in a significant way.

51. Walzer, *Thick and Thin*, 4, 18.

52. Ibid., 6.

53. See Daniel C. Maguire, *Sacred Energies: When the World's Religions Sit Down to Talk
about the Future of Human Life and the Plight of This Planet* (Minneapolis: Fortress, 2002),
and Paul F. Knitter and Chandra Muzaffar, eds., *Subverting Greed: Religious Perspectives on*

the Global Economy (Maryknoll, NY: Orbis, 2002). Two books that pioneered this discussion are Hans Küng, ed., *Yes to a Global Ethic* (New York: Continuum, 1996), and Leonard Swidler, ed., *For All Life: Toward a Universal Declaration of a Global Ethic: An Interreligious Dialogue* (Ashland, OR: White Cloud Press, 1998).

54. Walzer, *Thick and Thin*, 67–68.

CHAPTER 7: OMNIPOTENCE AND PREEMPTION

1. As Richard W. Van Alstyne has written: "In reality, . . . the United States possesses the attributes of monarchy; and it is through the President, the elective king, that it exerts its sovereign will among the family of nations. William H. Seward, Lincoln's Secretary of State, saw all this at a glance . . . and said: 'We elect a king for four years, and give him absolute power within certain limits, which after all he can interpret for himself'" (Von Alstyne, *The Rising American Empire* [New York: W. W. Norton, 1960], 6).

2. Edward Said, "The Nation Is Not United: The Other America," 3. *CounterPunch* (online journal), March 21, 2003.

3. President Bush, in his address at West Point in 2002, declared, "America has, and intends to keep, military strengths beyond challenge, thereby making the destabilizing arms races of other eras pointless, and limiting rivalries to trade and pursuits of peace" ("Remarks by the President at 2002 Graduation Exercise of the United States Military Academy, West Point, New York," Office of the Press Secretary, June 1, 2002). My argument will not preclude the possible defensive necessity of forms of preemptive strike, *if* "imminent danger" were to be actually established.

4. Reinhold Niebuhr, *The Irony of American History* (New York: Charles Scribner's Sons, 1952), 38.

5. Ibid., 24.

6. President Bush, 2002 State of the Union Address; quoted in "Bush & God," *Newsweek*, March 10, 2003.

7. See Catherine Keller, "The Armageddon of 9/11: A Counter-Apocalyptic Meditation," in *Strike Terror No More: Theology, Ethics, and the New War*, ed. Jon Berquist (St. Louis: Chalice, 2002). For an analysis of the theopolitics of the book of Revelation, see my *Apocalypse Now and Then: A Feminist Guide to the End of the World* (Boston: Beacon, 1996). See also my *God and Power: Counter-Apocalyptic Journeys* (Minneapolis: Augsburg-Fortress, 2005).

8. Alfred North Whitehead, *Process and Reality*, Corrected Edition, ed. David Ray Griffin and Donald W. Sherburne (New York: Free Press, 1978), 342.

9. Raymund of Aguiles, July 15, 1099, quoted in August C. Krey, *The First Crusade: The Accounts of Eye-Witnesses and Participants* (Princeton, NJ, and London: Princeton University Press, 1921), 261–62. For a more readable account of the Crusades and the other Abrahamic forms of messianic militarism, see Karen Armstrong, *Holy Wars: The Crusades and Their Impact on Today's World* (New York: Knopf Publishing Group, 2001).

10. Rahul Mahajan, *New Crusade: America's War on Terrorism* (New York: Monthly Review Press, 2002), 104.

11. Cited in Niall Ferguson's informatively proimperial text, *Empire: The Rise and Demise of the British World Order and the Lessons for Global Power* (New York: Basic Books, 2002), 7.

12. According to Richard Falk in *The Great Terror War* (Northampton, MA: Olive Branch Press, 2003), a self-contradictory synthesis is being attempted between the territorial force of patriotic nationalism and the nonterritorial thrust of the economic globalization, which it serves.

13. Lawrence F. Kaplan and William Kristol, *The War over Iraq: Saddam's Tyranny and America's Mission* (San Francisco: Encounter Books, 2003), 109–11.

14. On the U.S. government's nefarious role in these (and many other countries), see William Blum, *Killing Hope: U.S. Military and CIA Interventions since World War II* (Monroe, ME: Common Courage, 1995).

15. Kaplan and Kristol, *The War over Iraq*, 115.

16. Ibid., 3.

17. Niebuhr, *The Irony of American History*, 143.

18. Tariq Ali, *The Clash of Fundamentalisms: Crusades, Jihads, and Modernity* (London: Verso, 2002), 1. "Politically," says Ali, "the United States decided early on to use the tragedy [9/11] as a moral lever to re-map the world" (xiii).

19. David Ray Griffin, *God, Power, and Evil: A Process Theodicy* (Philadelphia: Westminster, 1976; reprint with new preface, Louisville, KY: Westminster John Knox, 2004).

20. John Calvin, *Institutes of the Christian Religion,* 3.23.1; 1.18.1.

21. *National Security Strategy of the United States of America*, September 17, 2002 (*http://www.whitehouse.gov/nsc/nss.html*).

22. Calvin, *Institutes*, 3.12.1.

23. Kaplan and Kristol, *The War over Iraq,* 3. The logic of foreign policy expert Joshua Muravchick is revealing: "A policeman gets his assignments from higher authority, but in the community of nations there is no authority higher than America" (cited with approval in Kaplan and Kristol, 121). This is a vision that Calvin would have denounced as idolatry—precisely for its aping of the omnipotent authority.

24. Calvin, *Institutes*, 3.13.7.

25. Ibid., 1.7.8.

26. Kaplan and Kristol, *The War over Iraq*, 123.

27. Niebuhr, *Irony*, 50.

28. Calvin, as quoted by Niebuhr (*Irony,* 51), who is considering Max Weber's interpretation of Calvinism in *The Protestant Ethic and the Spirit of Capitalism*.

29. From "New England's True Interest," by president William Stoughton of Yale University, cited by Niebuhr in *Irony,* 51.

30. Niebuhr, *Irony*, 146.

31. Whitehead, *Process and Reality,* 342.

32. David Ray Griffin, *God, Power, and Evil*, and *Evil Revisited*.

33. Introductory versions of these movements in theology include John B. Cobb Jr. and David Ray Griffin, *Process Theology: An Introductory Exposition*; Charles Hartshorne, *Omnipotence and Other Theological Mistakes*; Marjorie Suchocki, *God, Christ, Church*; Sallie McFague, *The Body of God; Super, Natural Christians*; Yvone Gebara, *Yearning for Running Waters*; Rosemary Ruether, *Sexism and God-Talk*; Catherine Keller, *From a Broken Web: Separation, Sexism, and Self*; Rita Nakashima Brock*, Journeys by Heart: A Christology of Erotic Power*; Karen Baker-Fletcher*, Sisters of Dust, Sisters of Spirit: Womanist Wordings on God and Creation*.

34. Richard Falk, *Religion and Humane Global Governance* (New York: Palgrave, 2001). Articulating the resistance to "globalization from above" pursued by transnational corporations, the World Bank, and other neoliberal free-trade instruments backed by the U.S. military, Falk's "globalization from below" is akin to what many are calling "democratic cosmopolitanism." It comprises social justice movements, alternative transnational formations, NGOs, the religious left, and environmental groups.

35. I have tried to elaborate certain spiritual and scriptural relations between uncertainty, courage, chaos, and creation in *Face of the Deep: A Theology of Becoming* (London: Routledge, 2003).

36. A version of this essay is published as chapter 2 of *God and Power: Counter-Apocalyptic Journeys* (Minneapolis: Augsburg-Fortress, 2005).

CHAPTER 8: COMMONWEALTH AND EMPIRE

1. See *http://www.newamericancentury.org*.

2. See Karl Jaspers, *The Origin and Goal of History* (New Haven, CT; Yale University Press, 1953). See also Lewis Mumford, *The Transformations of Man* (New York: Harper & Bros., 1956).

3. See Rudolf Bultmann, *Jesus and the Word* (New York: Scribner's, 1958) and *Jesus Christ and Mythology* (New York: Scribner's, 1958).

4. Alfred North Whitehead, *Adventures of Ideas* (New York: Free Press, 1967), 17–20.

CHAPTER 9: RESURRECTION AND EMPIRE

1. Susan P. Mattern, *Rome and the Enemy: Imperial Strategy in the Principate* (Berkeley: University of California Press, 1999), 90.

2. Richard A. Horsley, *Jesus and Empire: The Kingdom of God and the New World Disorder* (Minneapolis: Fortress, 2003), 117, 172.

3. Mattern, *Rome and the Enemy*, 22, 117.

4. See George McT. Kahin, *Intervention: How American Became Involved in Vietnam* (Garden City, NY: Anchor Press/Doubleday, 1987), 245, 360; Marilyn B. Young, *The Vietnam Wars 1945–1990* (New York: HarperCollins, 1991), 110, 137, 237, 324–25; Gabriel Kolko, *Anatomy of a War: Vietnam, the United States, and the Modern Historical Experience* (New York: Pantheon Books, 1985), 112–13, 164, 324, 341–42; and Robert Gallucci, *Neither Peace nor Honor: The Politics of American Military Policy in Viet Nam* (Baltimore: Johns Hopkins Press, 1975).

5. Horsley, *Jesus and Empire*, 29.

6. Ibid., 27.

7. Pseudo-Quintilian, *Declamations* 274.

8. Young, *The Vietnam Wars*, 137.

9. Kahin, *Intervention*, 283.

10. Horsley, *Jesus and Empire*, 6, 15, 28; Richard A. Horsley and Neil Asher Silberman, *The Message and the Kingdom: How Jesus and Paul Ignited a Revolution and Transformed the Ancient World* (New York: Grosset/Putnam, 1997), 84–86.

11. Horsley, *Jesus and Empire*, 129.

12. Ibid., 132.

13. 1 Cor. 15:44.

14. Gregory Riley, *Resurrection Reconsidered: Thomas and John in Controversy* (Minneapolis: Fortress, 1995).

15. John B. Cobb Jr., "The Resurrection of the Soul," *Harvard Theological Review* 80/2 (1987): 213–27.

16. See my *Parapsychology, Philosophy, and Spirituality: A Postmodern Exploration* (Albany: State University of New York Press, 1997).

17. Quoted in Horsley, *Jesus and Empire*, 23–24. The Greek word *euangelion* is, of course, the term used in the New Testament for "good news" or "gospel."

18. Quoted in G. Clarke Chapman, *Facing the Nuclear Heresy: A Call to Reformation* (Elgin, IL: Brethren Press, 1986), 50. Chapman's book is a call for Christians to declare nuclear weapons a *status confessionis*. My own view, however, is that nuclear weapons are now part and parcel of the world order based around sovereign states, so that the only way to eliminate the world of nuclear weapons is to overcome this world order through the creation of global democracy.

19. See Gernot Köhler, *Global Apartheid* (New York: Institute for World Order, 1978); Titus Alexander, *Unraveling Global Apartheid: An Overview of World Politics* (Cambridge: Polity Press, 1996); Richard A. Falk, *On Humane Governance: Toward a New Global Politics* (University Park: Pennsylvania State University Press, 1995), 49–55.

20. George F. Kennan, "Review of Current Trends: U.S. Foreign Policy," in *Documents on American Policy and Strategy, 1945–1950*, ed. Thomas H. Entzold and John Lewis Gaddis (New York: Columbia University Press), 226–28, at 226–27.